Step by Step
Card Play in No Trumps

Robert Berthe and
Norbert Lébely

Translated by
Barry Seabrook

B. T. Batsford Ltd, *London*

First published 1981

Reprinted and Revised 1996

© Robert Berthe and Norbert Lébely 1981

ISBN 0 7134 8051 3

A CIP catalogue record for this book is available from the British Library.

Typeset by Apsbridge Services Ltd, Nottingham.
Printed by Redwood Books, Trowbridge, Wiltshire
for the publishers,
B. T. Batsford Ltd, 4 Fitzhardinge Street,
London W1H 0AH

A BATSFORD BRIDGE BOOK
Series Editor: Tony Sowter

CONTENTS

Foreword   4
Preface   5

PART I
    Deals 1-48   8

PART II
    General Reference Section   106

PART III
    Exercises A-R   108

One Final Word   144

FOREWORD

Within the ranks of French experts, Robert Berthe is one whose study of bridge is among the most complete and most methodical He is certainly an author who is excellent at explaining how the play of the hand unfolds, since he is constantly aware of all declarer's problems

His talent and clarity of expression have made this work a very valuable teaching source, yet in spite of the great care he has expended on each analysis, this work might not have been quite complete without the collaboration of Norbert Lebely.

This little book will, I hope, be the first of a series to which we all look forward expectantly.

José le Dentu

PREFACE

Our aim has been to effect an original approach in the field of apprenticeship to card-play. Thus we cannot recommend too strongly a close study of this foreword.

Firstly, the framework is composed of three parts:

- The first comprises about fifty deals inviting you to discover the various manoeuvres applicable to the play at no trumps. We are especially insistent on the term 'discovery', and with this in view, we have appended two complementary techniques.

  (a) We have not divided the selected deals into artificial family groups, for you must acquire the habit of discovering for yourself the. technique appropriate for the particular deal with which you are confronted: similarly, we have intentionally avoided introducing each example with a label; what is there left to discover when the author gives an advance insight such as: 'Now then, this hand deals with a 'delayed-duck' or 'throw-in' ...?'

The deals are presented to you as they are, under conditions as near as possible to those you will meet at the table. Even so, we obviously had to classify the deals, and we therefore opted for 'ascending difficulty'.

  (b) Every declarer must ask himself a certain number of questions if he wishes to formulate a coherent plan, and using this basic approach as a point of departure we have chosen to employ the 'step-by-step' technique which will help you to rationalise through the process of question and answer, and then to operate your plan according to the various deductions you have made.

The commentary for each deal concludes with the formula entitled:

Guiding Principle

- The second section represents a cross-roads; in it you will find a succinct resume of the various techniques relative to the play at no trumps and accompanying each subject-heading will be found reference numbers for the relevant deals.

* Part III is composed of exercises; these are classified also in order of ascending difficulty, and they will help you to test the range of your knowledge and, we hope, of your progress.

Finally, a brief word on planning the play at no trumps.

You will notice that a similar question recurs at the top of each of the analyses: 'How many tricks do you have?' Herein lies the initial phase of your plan, and we do stress the fact that initially your count must not include tricks which are only potential, otherwise with:

♠ 432
♡ 98
♢ 10632
♣ 7654

♠ KQ
♡ KQJ10
♢ KQJ
♣ KQJ10

... you could claim, whereas you have four aces to knock out!

The establishment of the tricks which you are lacking will take into account the following factors:

1. The number of times you have to give up the lead;
2. The danger hand;
3. The number of entries at your disposal;
4. Suit-blockages, etc.

One last important detail: you are not expected to make the maximum number of tricks, as would be normal in a pairs contest, but to make sure of your contract as best you can, as though you were playing teams or rubber bridge.

Our main desire is that you should derive pleasure from our instruction and we trust that you will not be disappointed.

Robert Berthe and Norbert Lébely

PART I
DEALS 1-48

Deal No. 1

Dealer South. Game All.

> ♠ 8743
> ♡ 43
> ◇ AQ5
> ♣ K1087

> ♠ AK6
> ♡ A108
> ◇ K93
> ♣ QJ96

Lead: ♡5

South	West	North	East
1♣	Pass	1♠	Pass
1NT	Pass	2NT	Pass
3NT	All Pass		

How many winners do you have?
2 in spades, 1 in hearts, 3 in diamonds = 6 tricks.

Where will you find the three missing tricks?
In clubs, by knocking out the ace.

Each time you undertake a no trump contract you are confronted by a problem. What is it?
You have to ask yourself whether you should win the lead immediately or duck, and if the latter, how many times.

Why is this important?
Because it will determine the success or failure of many contracts. By holding up correctly, you will be cutting the communications between your opponents.

Consider the various distributions of the suit led:
In hearts there are eight cards missing:

(a) If the hearts are 4-4, East/West will make only four tricks in any event: three hearts and the ace of clubs. Holding up will therefore not have gained anything, but neither will it have cost.

(b) If the hearts are 5-3, the length being presumably with West, and you are careful to duck twice, East, holding the ace of clubs, will be. unable to give his partner the lead. The hold-up will thus have exhausted the communications between your two adversaries.

NB. It must be pointed out that if West has the ace of clubs the contract is unmakeable.

The Full Deal

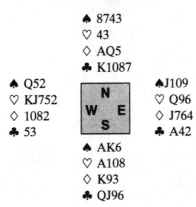

```
                    ♠ 8743
                    ♡ 43
                    ◇ AQ5
                    ♣ K1087
    ♠ Q52              N            ♠ J109
    ♡ KJ752                         ♡ Q96
    ◇ 1082      W          E        ◇ J764
    ♣ 53                            ♣ A42
                        S
                    ♠ AK6
                    ♡ A108
                    ◇ K93
                    ♣ QJ96
```

Guiding Principle

In no trumps the technique known as the hold-up is fundamental, for if one of your opponents possesses an established suit it is essential that his partner should not be able to reach his hand.

For this purpose we advise you to employ the Rule of 7:

Whenever you possess only one guard in the suit led and envisage giving up the lead only once, count the number of cards you hold in that suit between your two hands, subtract the total from 7, and the answer will be the number of times you require to duck; thus in the foregoing example, there were two hearts in dummy plus three in hand = 5; 7-5 = 2, therefore the Rule of 7 confirms that it was necessary to hold up twice.

Deal No. 2

Dealer South. Game All.

♠ K3
♡ Q52
◇ KJ987
♣ 654

♠ A64
♡ AJ
◇ 1053
♣ AKQJ10

Lead: ♠5

South	West	North	East
1♣	Pass	1◇	Pass
3NT	All Pass		

What is your winner count?
2 in spades, 1 in hearts, 5 in clubs = 8 tricks.

How will you establish the extra tricks?
In diamonds, if either the ace or queen is favourably placed and you guess correctly which one to play from dummy on the first round.

Is there the possibility of establishing a trick elsewhere? If so, what is it?
Yes, in hearts, if East has the king.

Can you succeed even if West has the king of hearts?
Of course; you need only play the ace followed by the knave without bothering about the position of the king.

Are you going to duck the first round of spades?
No. You must be careful to preserve the king of spades as an entry to the established queen of hearts. You have a second spade stopper and you have to give up the lead only once to your opponents. If you duck at Trick 1 the opponents will continue spades. Your only sure communication with the dummy will have evaporated prematurely and you will have to resort to the heart finesse, whereas the suggested line of play makes that finesse pointless.

So win the first trick with the ace of spades and continue with the ace and knave of hearts, thus making your contract 100 per cent certain.

The Full Deal

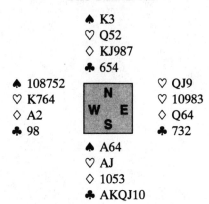

```
                    ♠ K3
                    ♡ Q52
                    ◇ KJ987
                    ♣ 654
    ♠ 108752                      ♡ QJ9
    ♡ K764          N             ♡ 10983
    ◇ A2        W       E         ◇ Q64
    ♣ 98            S             ♣ 732
                    ♠ A64
                    ♡ AJ
                    ◇ 1053
                    ♣ AKQJ10
```

Guiding Principle

Always count your certain tricks and ask yourself how many you have to establish. Do not make an automatic dash for your longest suit, for there may be a winning line of play against any distribution and any defence. Make a close study of your entry problems: lack of reflection at Trick 1 can often prove costly later.

Deal No. 3

Dealer East. Game All.

♠ 752
♡ 854
◇ 32
♣ K7653

♠ K83
♡ AJ6
◇ A974
♣ A42

Lead: ♠6 East plays the knave

South	West	North	East
–	–	–	Pass
1NT	All Pass		

How many sure tricks do you have?
1 in spades (after the lead), 1 in hearts, 1 in diamonds, 2 in clubs = 5 certain tricks.

After winning the first spade with the king how will you set about finding the two extra tricks? What conditions must be satisfied?
From the club suit, and this must be divided 3-2.

What problem are you faced with?
Apart from the king of clubs the dummy has no other entry, and if you play ace, king and another club, you will certainly set up two tricks but you will not be in a position to benefit from them.

What technique must you apply?
You must duck a club in both hands, either on the first or second round of the suit. By proceeding thus, you will have maintained communications in your established suit.

The Full Deal

```
                 ♠ 752
                 ♡ 854
                 ◇ 32
                 ♣ K7653
  ♠ AQ1064      ┌─────┐      ♠ J9
  ♡ K93         │  N  │      ♡ Q1072
  ◇ 1085        │W   E│      ◇ KQJ6
  ♣ Q10         │  S  │      ♣ J98
                 └─────┘
                 ♠ K83
                 ♡ AJ6
                 ◇ A974
                 ♣ A42
```

Guiding Principle

This type of duck is a frequent ploy. While it is indispensable to compensate for the lack of entries, it may equally well be employed in order to verify the distribution of a particular suit without losing control. Thus with some holding like Kxx opposite Axxx, there is no question of establishing two immediate tricks for the defence. Perhaps the outstanding cards are 3-3; an initial duck in the suit will allow you to find out.

Deal No. 4

Dealer North. Game All

♠ KQ32
♡ K3
◇ AK982
♣ 86

♠ A4
♡ A7542
◇ 5
♣ QJ1092

Lead: ♠J

South	West	North	East
–	–	1◇	Pass
1♡	Pass	1♠	Pass
2NT	Pass	3NT	All Pass

Count your tricks before calling for dummy's first card.
3 in spades, 2 in hearts, 2 in diamonds = 7 tricks. You require 2 more.

Which suit will you elect to establish?
The defensive opening not being immediately threatening, your choice lies between hearts and clubs. Naturally you choose the club suit, for in order to satisfy your trick requirements it would be imperative that the hearts should break 3-3, which is only a 36 per cent chance.

How many entries to your hand will you require?
You must foresee that the enemy will refuse the first round of clubs; consequently you will need two entries: one to remove the second top club (ace or king), and a second to allow you access to the established suit.

What are those two entries?
The ace of hearts and the ace of spades.

So which of dummy's cards do you contribute to Trick 1?
When you have a holding such as Ax opposite KQxx it is normal to begin with the ace, and then to play towards the two honours in order to avoid any blockage. However, you must certainly have realised that in the

present example you must preserve the ace as an entry to your hand. Only by doing this will you be sure of establishing the club suit. You therefore take care to play the king on the opening lead. In this way you will be in hand when your opponents continue with spades and you will score ten tricks.

The Full Deal

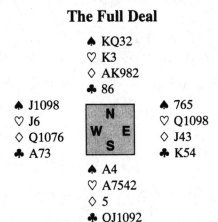

```
                    ♠ KQ32
                    ♡ K3
                    ◇ AK982
                    ♣ 86
    ♠ J1098                      ♠ 765
    ♡ J6              N          ♡ Q1098
    ◇ Q1076      W       E       ◇ J43
    ♣ A73            S           ♣ K54
                    ♠ A4
                    ♡ A7542
                    ◇ 5
                    ♣ QJ1092
```

Guiding Principle

Whether you are playing in no trumps or in a suit contract, always exercise maximum care over the preservation of entries in the hand requiring suit establishment. You will frequently possess some holding such as Ax opposite Kx. If the opponents lead this suit, win with the honour which will subsequently play no further entry role. Train yourself to handle your entries correctly.

Deal No. 5

Dealer South. Game All.

♠ A82
♡ K93
◇ J4
♣ J10765

♠ K43
♡ A75
◇ A103
♣ KQ94

Lead: ◇6

South	West	North	East
1♣	Pass	3♣	Pass
3NT	All Pass		

How many sure tricks do you have?
2 in spades, 2 in hearts, 1 in diamonds = 5 certain tricks.

Where will the extra tricks come from?
The club suit naturally; all you have to do is to knock out the ace.

Which of dummy's cards do you play at Trick 1?
You have nothing to gain by playing the knave, for if West has led away from king-queen, your ten will take the first trick.

On the other hand what advantage will you derive from playing the four at Trick 1 in any event?
(i)   If East plays a small diamond your ten will win the trick.

(ii) If East produces a high honour, by winning with the ace you will have created a second stop in the enemy suit.

For what precise reason is your contract assured?
Because you only need to abandon the lead once. The problem would be quite different had you been obliged to give up the lead twice.

The Full Deal

```
                 ♠ A82
                 ♡ K93
                 ◇ J4
                 ♣ J10765
 ♠ Q97          ┌─────────┐      ♠ J1065
 ♡ J642         │    N    │      ♡ Q108
 ◇ K9865        │ W     E │      ◇ Q72
 ♣ A            │    S    │      ♣ 832
                └─────────┘
                 ♠ K43
                 ♡ A75
                 ◇ A103
                 ♣ KQ94
```

Guiding Principle

It would be extremely unwise to duck a queen or king with the following holdings:

Jxx	10x	xx
A10	AJx	AJ10

… where your intention is to give up the lead only once.

Deal No. 6

Dealer South. Love All.

♠ K54
♡ A762
◇ 743
♣ A84

♠ A63
♡ QJ54
◇ AK8
♣ K72

Lead: ♠Q

South	West	North	East
1NT	Pass	3NT	All Pass

When the dummy goes down you have cause to congratulate partner for opting for the no trumps. You would have four certain losers in four hearts.

How many sure tricks do you have?
2 in spades, 1 in hearts, 2 in diamonds, 2 in clubs = 7 tricks. You have to find two more.

Which suit will furnish those tricks?
The only viable suit is hearts.

How will you play the suit?
(i)   If it breaks 3-2, you have only to worry about the position of the king and consequently you will make your contract with ease.

(ii) However, you will have realised that we are trying to increase your sense of foresight by asking this question, and so you should give some thought to a 4-1 division. After all, a 28 per cent frequency is not negligible.

So, how will you set about it?
If West has four to the king you cannot avoid going down. On the other hand if it is East who has them you merely need to play twice towards your queen-knave.

You may also profit from a small additional chance. What is it?
Guard against a singleton king with West by cashing the ace first, the dummy has sufficient entries.

Are you going to duck the opening lead?
There is no point: you have two spade stops and you intend to give up the lead only once. Therefore:

(a) Ace of spades and four of hearts to the ace (the king does not appear).

(b) Small heart to your queen which holds, West discarding.

(c) Two of clubs to the ace.

(d) Small heart towards your knave; East cannot prevent you from making three heart tricks and thus your game.

The Full Deal

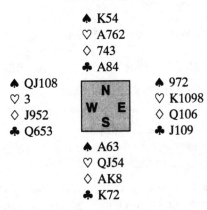

```
                  ♠ K54
                  ♡ A762
                  ◇ 743
                  ♣ A84
  ♠ QJ108                      ♠ 972
  ♡ 3          N               ♡ K1098
  ◇ J952    W     E            ◇ Q106
  ♣ Q653       S               ♣ J109
                  ♠ A63
                  ♡ QJ54
                  ◇ AK8
                  ♣ K72
```

Guiding Principle

Never rush blindly at a finesse which will not only fail to gain, but which runs the risk of costing a trick. Thus with:

	QJx	QJxx
or	▩	▩
	Axxx	Axx

lead small towards dummy's honours.

Deal No. 7

Dealer East. North/South Game.

♠ Q43
♡ K8
◇ QJ987
♣ QJ2

♠ A62
♡ A3
◇ 1054
♣ AK1073

Lead: ♡Q

South	West	North	East
–	–	–	Pass
1NT	Pass	3NT	All Pass

How many immediate tricks can you count?
1 in spades, 2 in hearts, 5 in clubs = 8 tricks. You need one more.

In which suit do you intend to find it?
It is very tempting to go for the diamonds, for you have only to dislodge the ace and king in order to find three tricks.

However, this line is doomed to failure. For what reason?
Your opponents have attacked a suit in which you have only two stops; the ace and king. They have nine cards in that suit and except in the highly improbable case of a 7-2 break with both the top diamonds with East or a blockage, they have no communications problems. If you set about establishing your longest suit, you will have to give up the lead twice at a time when you have only one heart stopper remaining. clearly, the opponents will gather three or four heart tricks plus the ace and king of diamonds, for the lead has conferred upon them an undeniable advantage in the race for suit-establishment.

Is there any hope of success? What is it?
Yes, you must hope that the king of spades is favourably placed (we won't insult you by asking you which opponent must have it).

So proceed with the play accordingly:

Win the opening lead with the ace of hearts and immediately play the two of spades towards the queen; West goes up with the king and continues with the four of hearts. Just take your seven other tricks: queen and ace of spades and five clubs.

This line of play was a mere 50 per cent (favourable position of the king of spades), but there was no other winning line.

The Full Deal

♠ Q43
♡ K8
◇ QJ987
♣ QJ2

♠ K108
♡ QJ974
◇ K62
♣ 95

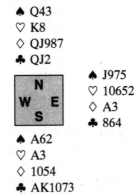

♠ J975
♡ 10652
◇ A3
♣ 864

♠ A62
♡ A3
◇ 1054
♣ AK1073

Guiding Principle

Always count the number of tricks you require carefully, and never embark automatically on an attractive-looking suit without taking the time-factor into consideration. Ask yourself whether your winners in the suit led are sufficient in number for you to give up the lead a certain number of times.

Deal No. 8

Dealer North. East/West Game.

♠ 1095
♡ A8743
◇ 95
♣ Q109

♠ A84
♡ 52
◇ KQJ106
♣ AKJ

Lead: ♠6

South	West	North	East
–	–	Pass	Pass
1◇	Pass	1♡	Pass
1NT(i)	Pass	2♣(ii)	Pass
2NT(iii)	Pass	3NT	All Pass

(i)   15-18
(ii) Crowhurst
(iii) Maximum, without three-card heart fit and ruffing-value

How many immediate tricks do you have?
1 in spades, 1 in hearts, 3 in clubs = 5 certain tricks and you can set up four diamonds by knocking out the ace.

At Trick 1, East plays the knave of spades.

Will you duck the opening lead and if you do, how many times?
You will not have failed to bear in mind the Rule of 7. You possess 3+3 = 6 cards in spades: 7–6 = 1; you will therefore duck once only and win the second round of spades.

What in fact will happen if you duck the second round of spades?
If he has no entry or if the spades are 4-3 West will switch to a heart, a suit in which you only have one stopper. (Remember that the opponents know

from the bidding that you have only two cards in hearts.) After taking the ace of spades you will establish the diamonds, hoping that the ace is not in the same hand as the long spades.

If the spades are 4-3, you will lose three spades and the ace of diamonds. East wins the second diamond and exits with a heart. Your contract is home with one spade, one heart, four diamonds and three clubs.

The Full Deal

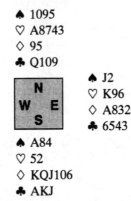

```
              ♠ 1095
              ♡ A8743
              ◇ 95
              ♣ Q109
  ♠ KQ763              ♠ J2
  ♡ QJ10       N       ♡ K96
  ◇ 74      W     E    ◇ A832
  ♣ 872        S       ♣ 6543
              ♠ A84
              ♡ 52
              ◇ KQJ106
              ♣ AKJ
```

Guiding Principle

Do not overlook the advantages of ducking and systematically apply the Rule of 7. In this way you will effectively counter any switch by the defence.

Deal No. 9

Dealer South. East/West Game.

 ♠ 932
 ♡ 853
 ◇ KJ5
 ♣ AQ84

 ♠ KJ5
 ♡ AQ
 ◇ Q872
 ♣ KJ102

Lead: ♡J

South	West	North	East
1NT	Pass	3NT	All Pass

Top tricks?

2 in hearts (the knave is covered by the king and ace and you have one further winner in the suit), 4 in clubs = 6 tricks. You need to find three more.

In which suit?

Diamonds naturally. If the suit should divide 3-3, you will make three tricks in it after removing the ace. If it breaks 4-2, the most probable division (48 per cent), what precaution should you take?

Lead twice towards dummy's combined honour holding.

Why?

Imagine that West has Ax. If you manoeuvre correctly you will make three tricks, whereas if you play from dummy you will have sacrificed one of your honours to no good purpose.

Therefore, at Trick 2, play the two of diamonds towards the knave, which holds.

What now?

A club to your hand and a further diamond towards the table: West plays the ace and your objective has been attained.

The Full Deal

```
              ♠ 932
              ♡ 853
              ◇ KJ5
              ♣ AQ84
♠ AQ8                      ♠ 10764
♡ J10972      N            ♡ K64
◇ A4       W     E         ◇ 10963
♣ 953         S            ♣ 76
              ♠ KJ5
              ♡ AQ
              ◇ Q872
              ♣ KJ102
```

Guiding Principle

You will frequently be faced with combined honour holdings such as:

QJxx

Kxx

Apply the principle of playing twice towards the two honours provided you have sufficient entries.

Deal No. 10

Dealer East. East/West Game.

```
                    ♠ 1098
                    ♡ 1094
                    ◇ AKJ5
                    ♣ J102
```

```
                    ♠ KQJ5
                    ♡ KQJ
                    ◇ 942
                    ♣ KQ6
```

Lead: ◇7 (4th best)

South	West	North	East
–	–	–	Pass
1NT	Pass	3NT	All Pass

How many sure tricks?

In spite of the 26 points your trick-total in hardly impressive, and for the moment you are looking at only two certain tricks, in diamonds. (On this point, a reminder of that basic principle: never count potential winners as sure tricks.)

Where are you going to find the seven missing tricks?

In the three other suits, by knocking out their respective aces.

If the diamond length is with West as the lead shows, the contract seems to be in no danger. You have seven cards in this suit, headed by AK4 and the queen is probably right.

Now what card do you play from dummy at Trick 1; a top honour, the knave, or the five?

Before deciding, it might be as well if we consider together the inferences of this fourth best lead. Originally, this conventional lead was invented to help defenders, but declarer can also gather useful information from it. Let us take a closer look: you subtract the numerical value of the card led from 11 and the answer is the total number of cards higher than the lead possessed by the other three hands. Therefore deduct 7 from 11 and you obtain the answer 4. Now you hold ace, king, knave and nine which rank above the seven.

What inference do you draw from this very simple calculation?
East possesses no card higher than the seven. Consequently it is not one of dummy's honours that you must select at Trick 1 but the five. East duly plays the six and you take the trick with the nine. Later you will finesse against West's queen and make four tricks in the suit. In this way you will simply give up three aces to the defence since you still retain three guards in the suit led initially. Thanks to your correct interpretation of the lead you will make the contract with an overtrick.

The Full Deal

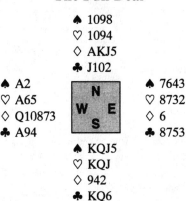

```
              ♠ 1098
              ♡ 1094
              ◇ AKJ5
              ♣ J102
  ♠ A2                      ♠ 7643
  ♡ A65          N          ♡ 8732
  ◇ Q10873    W   E         ◇ 6
  ♣ A94          S          ♣ 8753
              ♠ KQJ5
              ♡ KQJ
              ◇ 942
              ♣ KQ6
```

NB. It is easy to check that good defence (refusal to allow you to slip through an early heart or club trick) will beat you if you play one of dummy's honours at Trick 1. In effect you will have to knock out West's three aces but meanwhile the latter will have established two long diamonds.

Guiding Principle

Do not overlook the important information furnished by a lead of the fourth best, and refer systematically to the Rule of 11. However, bear in mind that the card led will furnish different information according to its numerical value:

(i) A high card (6-8) will reveal the whereabouts of the outstanding honours in the suit, as in the example described above.

(ii) A low card, a 2, 3 or a 4, with the lower cards visible in the latter two cases, will on the other hand give an indication of the distribution, for it will probably be from just a four-card suit.

Deal No. 11

Dealer South. East/West Game.

♠ K8
♡ 872
◇ A103
♣ AJ1096

♠ A95
♡ KQ5
◇ K842
♣ Q32

Lead: ♡6

South	West	North	East
1NT	Pass	3NT	All Pass

How many immediate tricks?
2 in spades, 1 in hearts (after the lead), 2 in diamonds, 1 in clubs = 6 tricks. Three more are required and these will be provided by the long club suit.

What inference do you draw from the lead? How many cards does East have higher than the six (4th best)?
The Rule of 11 shows that he holds only one card higher than the six. It might be the ace, but in that case West would have led the top of his sequence J1096x. Therefore East's higher card will be the nine, ten or knave.

In fact, East contributes the knave. Now you possess KQx opposite three small.

Where is the danger on this hand?
In order to enjoy the clubs you will take the club finesse. If West has the king all will be well but if East has the king he will take it and play back a heart. If you have taken the first trick you will then be in danger of losing a club and four heart tricks.

Is there a better way?

Yes, you must duck the knave of hearts. One of two things will happen:

(a) Either the hearts will divide 5-2 and West will be unable to regain the lead; or

(b) East can return a heart and the suit will have broken 4-3. You will then lose only three hearts and the king of clubs.

The Full Deal

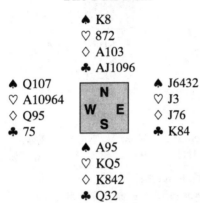

        ♠ K8
        ♡ 872
        ◇ A103
        ♣ AJ1096

♠ Q107   ♠ J6432
♡ A10964   ♡ J3
◇ Q95   ◇ J76
♣ 75   ♣ K84

        ♠ A95
        ♡ KQ5
        ◇ K842
        ♣ Q32

Guiding Principle

KQx is equivalent to an ace. You must duck with this honour holding whenever you fear that your right-hand opponent may gain the lead, for if this should prove to be the case, the prospect of retaining only Kx or Qx in the danger suit is scarcely a pleasant one.

Deal No. 12

Dealer South. East/West Game.

♠ A75
♡ 872
◇ AK83
♣ Q93

♠ K108
♡ KQ5
◇ 102
♣ AJ1085

Lead: ♡6

South	West	North	East
1NT	Pass	3NT	All Pass

How many immediate tricks?

2 in spades, 1 in hearts (after the lead), 2 in diamonds, 1 in clubs = 6 tricks. Three more are required and these will be provided by the club suit.

What inference do you draw from the lead?

Just as in Deal No. 11, West is marked with the ace of hearts and East plays the knave.

Do you duck the knave of hearts?

This was correct in Deal No. 11, but it would be wrong this time.

Why?

There is no danger of East gaining the lead to play a heart through your remaining doubleton honour because you can take the club finesse into the West hand.

If you duck the first heart, the defence will clear the suit and if West has the king of clubs he will cash two more heart winners after you have taken the club finesse and you will go down.

The Full Deal

```
                    ♠ A75
                    ♡ 872
                    ◇ AK83
                    ♣ Q93
    ♠ Q94          ┌─────────┐      ♠ J632
    ♡ A10964       │    N    │      ♡ J3
    ◇ 765          │  W   E  │      ◇ QJ94
    ♣ K2           │    S    │      ♣ 764
                   └─────────┘
                    ♠ K108
                    ♡ KQ5
                    ◇ 102
                    ♣ AJ1085
```

Guiding Principle

Whether we duck or not with KQx depends on who we fear getting the lead. If you cannot avoid allowing your right-hand opponent in, it is probably right to duck but if you can keep him off lead then win the trick immediately.

Deal No. 13

Dealer West. East/West Game.

> ♠ K104
> ♡ AK986
> ◇ K3
> ♣ 1052

> ♠ J92
> ♡ 752
> ◇ AQJ10
> ♣ K98

Lead: ♣3

South	West	North	East
	Pass	1♡	Pass
2◇	Pass	2♡	Pass
2NT	Pass	3NT	All Pass

East plays the queen of clubs; do you duck?
Obviously not, for you might fail to make a club trick at all. West probably has the ace and knave.

When you win with the king of clubs how many tricks do you have?
2 in hearts, 4 in diamonds, 1 in clubs = 7 certain tricks.

You have to establish two more. How will you do it?
(a) A 3-2 heart break (68 per cent) will furnish two tricks.

(b) If West has the queen of spades (successive finesses if necessary), that suit will provide two tricks 50 per cent of the time.

Which solution will you choose?
While the cultivation of percentage plays may normally constitute a sound habit, you must not forget that in no trump contracts, while it is essential to count your tricks in attack, you must not overlook those of the defence; in the present example the defence has already set up three club tricks after the lead (West's three, the two being visible, has shown that the suit is fortunately divided 4-3). The defenders can take the ace of spades at any

time. If you give up a heart trick to them in order to set up dummy's two long cards, they will rake in five tricks: three clubs + the ace of spades + a heart, and you will be defeated.

Therefore you must rely on the spade finesse.

So how do you proceed?
Play the knave of spades: East is forced to win with the ace and when he continues with a club West takes three clubs and exits with a heart. Naturally you win this trick.

How do you continue?
Play the king of diamonds, then three further rounds of the suit before taking another spade finesse.

The Full Deal

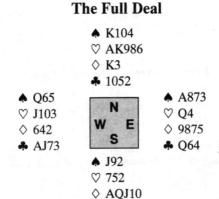

```
                ♠ K104
                ♡ AK986
                ◇ K3
                ♣ 1052
    ♠ Q65                      ♠ A873
    ♡ J103          N          ♡ Q4
    ◇ 642      W        E      ◇ 9875
    ♣ AJ73          S          ♣ Q64
                ♠ J92
                ♡ 752
                ◇ AQJ10
                ♣ K98
```

Guiding Principle

Do not be merely satisfied with counting those tricks which you require to establish; think about the defenders' tricks too; what is the point of setting up a ninth trick if meanwhile your opponents can run five?

Deal No. 14

Dealer North. East/West Game.

♠ 943
♡ 5
◇ AK10987
♣ A94

♠ AJ72
♡ AK73
◇ Q
♣ Q753

Lead: ♡Q

South	West	North	East
–	–	1◇	Pass
1♡	Pass	2◇	Pass
3NT	All Pass		

Count your tricks.
1 in spades, 2 in hearts, 3 in diamonds, 1 in clubs = 7 tricks. You need two more.

Where from?
The diamonds, obviously.

What is the normal way of playing this suit?
You cash the queen, then cross to the table with the ace of clubs and lead out your top diamonds.

However, have you noticed that the dummy will then be entryless? Therefore this line will fail if an opponent holds four or more diamonds to the knave.

What is the solution?
Overtake the queen of diamonds with the king and continue the suit until the knave appears. You may well have sacrificed a trick if the knave falls in three rounds, but if it does not, your ace of clubs will remain on the table as an entry to the established diamonds. You will have guaranteed nine tricks.

The Full Deal

```
              ♠ 943
              ♡ 5
              ◇ AK10987
              ♣ A94
  ♠ K1065      ┌─────────┐      ♠ Q8
  ♡ QJ109      │    N    │      ♡ 8642
  ◇ 43         │  W   E  │      ◇ J652
  ♣ K62        │    S    │      ♣ J108
              └─────────┘
              ♠ AJ72
              ♡ AK73
              ◇ Q
              ♣ Q753
```

Guiding Principle

If you are short of entries do not yield to the temptation of false economy: if you have a bare honour opposite a suit containing all the intermediates, such as AJ1098 opposite K, overtake the king with the ace and give up a trick to the queen.

Deal No. 15

Dealer East. Game All.

♠ 8
♡ A2
◇ 10654
♣ AJ8642

♠ AJ2
♡ QJ6
◇ AK3
♣ Q1093

Lead: ♠K

South	West	North	East
–	–	–	Pass
1NT	Pass	3NT	All Pass

How many tricks do you have?
1 in spades, 1 in hearts, 2 in diamonds, 1 in clubs = 5 tricks. You need 4 more.

Which suit will you set up?
The clubs, naturally, and you need only to capture or drop the king in order to establish sufficient tricks.

While it would therefore seem that the contract is in no danger the opening lead poses a problem. What is it?
East/West have nine spades between them. Suppose you win the first trick with the ace in order to preserve a guard in the suit with J2: if the guarded king of clubs is with East, the latter will return a spade and the contract will be in jeopardy.

What is the solution, then?
By refusing the first spade you will leave West on lead, thus preventing him from continuing with spades: should he insist, he will be playing into your AJ. You therefore apply the principle of ducking which has been effectively named the Bath Coup.

West gives you a suspicious glance and after a few moments' thought he switches to the seven of hearts.

What is your reaction? How should you reason it out?
Remember that four club tricks will suffice and that you do not require an extra trick in hearts.

Suppose you did try the heart finesse, what risk would you be running?
East might win the the king of hearts and return a spade before you had time to broach the clubs, and your Bath Coup at Trick 1 would have gained nothing. In fact you would go down an extra trick.

Consequently, do not be tempted by the heart finesse since your QJ still gives you a stopper in that suit.

Play the ace of hearts, then come to hand with the ace of diamonds in order to run the queen of clubs. The finesse fails but your contract is assured.

Thus there were two traps on this hand but doubtless you overcame them.

The Full Deal

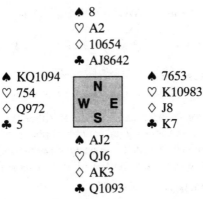

```
                    ♠ 8
                    ♡ A2
                    ◇ 10654
                    ♣ AJ8642
    ♠ KQ1094                      ♠ 7653
    ♡ 754            N            ♡ K10983
    ◇ Q972       W     E          ◇ J8
    ♣ 5             S             ♣ K7
                    ♠ AJ2
                    ♡ QJ6
                    ◇ AK3
                    ♣ Q1093
```

Guiding Principle

When you possess AJx in a suit and your left-hand opponent leads the king, you will gain a precious tempo by ducking. But be careful not to apply this technique blindly. The decision to duck or to win will depend on your chosen line of play.

Deal No. 16

Dealer South, Game All.

```
              ♠ K63
              ♡ A105
              ◇ AJ9
              ♣ J1083
```

```
                 N
              W     E
                 S
```

```
              ♠ A7
              ♡ K96
              ◇ Q1062
              ♣ AQ96
```

Lead: ♠4. East plays the ten

South	West	North	East
–	Pass	1◇	Pass
1NT	Pass	3NT	All Pass

Count up your sure tricks.
2 in spades, 2 in hearts, 1 in diamonds, 1 in clubs = 6 tricks.

You need to establish three extra tricks. If either the club or diamond finesses work you will make your contract without difficulty. However, you must have noticed that finesses rarely win in text-books, so you must find a way of succeeding however the adverse cards are placed.

Will you duck the lead?
The Rule of 7 (amended) is equally valid when you have two stoppers, provided that a switch is not immediately imminent. Therefore duck at Trick 1. East continues with the knave to West's two and your ace.

Which suit do you play on first, clubs or diamonds?
If the spades are 4-4, your order of play is of no great moment, but if they are 5-3, the length is certainly with West. You must therefore kill his potential entry by playing on clubs first. later, you can take the diamond finesse in safety: either the communications between East/West will have been severed (spades 5-3), or the spades will be 4-4 and the opponents will make two spades and two minor-suit kings.

So, how do you continue?

You cannot afford to cross to dummy in order to take the club finesse since West might win with the king of clubs and return a heart, establishing a fifth trick for the defence when the king of diamonds is wrong. Simply lay down the ace and queen of clubs.

The Full Deal

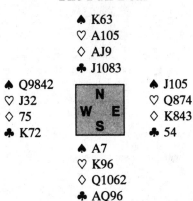

```
              ♠ K63
              ♡ A105
              ◇ AJ9
              ♣ J1083
♠ Q9842                      ♠ J105
♡ J32          N             ♡ Q874
◇ 75        W     E          ◇ K843
♣ K72          S             ♣ 54
              ♠ A7
              ♡ K96
              ◇ Q1062
              ♣ AQ96
```

Guiding Principle

Apply the Rule of 7 when you hold two guards in the suit led, and do not fear a switch. Furthermore, you must exercise care over the order in which you embark on your suit establishment. Your main consideration is to kill the potential entry in the hand you consider to be dangerous while still retaining a stopper in the suit.

Deal No. 17

Dealer South. Love All.

                    ♠ A764
                    ♡ Q92
                    ◇ Q5
                    ♣ 6542

                    ♠ K93
                    ♡ AJ105
                    ◇ A32
                    ♣ AK8

Lead: ◇6

South	West	North	East
1♣	Pass	1♠	Pass
2NT	Pass	3NT	All Pass

How many top tricks?
2 spades, 1 hearts, 1 diamonds, 2 clubs = 6 tricks. You require three more.

What are your prospects?
The only viable suit is hearts, for it will be possible to set up three extra tricks if East has the king.

Do you play the five or the queen of diamonds at Trick 1?
The queen, naturally; you must hope that West has led away from the king, and you will gain nothing by playing the five, for East will insert an intermediate card forcing your ace. The queen is covered by East's king.

Do you win immediately?
Since the success of the contract depends now on the favourable position of the king of hearts, there is no point in ducking.

How do you continue?
You cross to dummy with the ace of spades and play a heart.

Which card do you lead, the two, nine or queen?
You will not have failed to notice that you have no further communication with the table, so there is nothing to be gained by playing the two: you will not be able to repeat the finesse even if it wins. The queen seems to be the correct card to play since it will allow you to capture the king twice guarded.

However, what will happen if the king is three times guarded?
You will be unable to make four heart tricks since you will find yourself in one of the two following situations according to whether you have played the five or the ten from your hand: either:

92

AJ10

where you will be forced to win the next heart in your hand, East retaining the king still doubleton; or:

92

AJ5

when East will cover the nine with the king and retain 87 against your J5. There is only one correct card to play on broaching the hearts and that is the nine; you will contribute the 5 from your hand. That is followed by the queen for your ten, and finally the two towards your remaining tenace of AJ.

The Full Deal

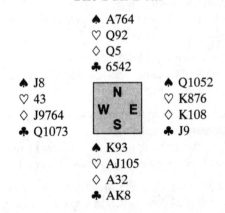

♠ A764
♡ Q92
◇ Q5
♣ 6542

♠ J8
♡ 43
◇ J9764
♣ Q1073

♠ Q1052
♡ K876
◇ K108
♣ J9

♠ K93
♡ AJ105
◇ A32
♣ AK8

Guiding Principle

Certain suit-combinations require text book handling and should be known to you. Recourse to these is indispensable whenever you have a dearth of communications.

Deal No. 18

Dealer South. East/West Game.

♠ J3
♡ 75
◇ QJ1065
♣ AQ103

♠ A95
♡ AJ4
◇ A93
♣ KJ52

Lead: ♡K. East plays the two

South	West	North	East
1NT	Pass	3NT	Pass

How many certain tricks do you have?
1 in spades, 1 in hearts, 1 in diamonds, 4 in clubs =7 tricks. You need two more.

Which you suit will you establish?
The diamonds; you will take the diamond finesse and whether or not this succeeds you will have enough tricks.

Do you remember a technique already put to use, and if so, do you apply it in the present example?
It would seem that this is an appropriate moment to remind you of the Bath Coup, but what will happen if you leave West on lead at Trick 1?

On seeing his partner's discouraging two, West will realise that you began with AJx and he will doubtless switch to a spade. You will have to allow East to hold this trick and he will switch back to hearts while the king of diamonds is still out. Therefore you will not resort to the Bath Coup on this occasion, but win at once with the ace of hearts. Your Jx will constitute a secondary guard since only West can regain the lead in diamonds and he is the non-dangerous opponent.

What now?
Cross to the table with a club and lead the queen of diamonds. When this holds you continue with the five on which East discards the seven of spades.

Do you take the ace or play the nine?
The ace, and then continue with the nine which West still does not capture. Do not forget to overtake with the ten and play another. There is no risk in setting up a tenth trick in diamonds since West cannot harm you.

The Full Deal

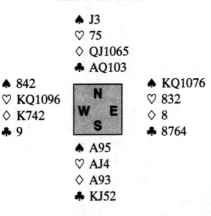

```
                    ♠ J3
                    ♡ 75
                    ◇ QJ1065
                    ♣ AQ103
    ♠ 842                        ♠ KQ1076
    ♡ KQ1096        N            ♡ 832
    ◇ K742       W     E         ◇ 8
    ♣ 9             S            ♣ 8764
                    ♠ A95
                    ♡ AJ4
                    ◇ A93
                    ♣ KJ52
```

Guiding Principle

Never allow technical knowledge to cloud your judgement and do not yield to the temptation to duck if you fear a dangerous switch.

Deal No. 19

Dealer South. East/West Game.

```
        ♠ AJ642
        ♡ 82
        ◇ K5
        ♣ A963
```

```
        ♠ 105
        ♡ AK6
        ◇ QJ107
        ♣ QJ102
```

Lead: ♡Q

South	West	North	East
1NT	Pass	2♡(i)	Pass
2♠	Pass	3♣	Pass
3NT	All Pass		

(i)   Transfer

Count your tricks.

1 in spades, 2 in hearts, 1 in clubs = 4 tricks. You need to set up five more.

Do you duck the opening lead?

Yes, for you do not fear a switch, quite the contrary, and you will be cutting the communications if the hearts are 5-3.

Now examine the various prospects offered by each suit:

(i)   *Spades:* These are strictly limited since in order to set up three extra tricks here, you would need to find KQx with West, any other lie of the cards would be unfavourable.

(ii) *Diamonds:* You can establish three tricks by knocking out the ace.

(iii) *Clubs:* You can establish two or three tricks according to the position of the king.

What conclusion do you draw from the analysis of these combined holdings?

No suit alone can produce the five required tricks, so ask yourself the following questions:

(i) Which suits will you choose?

(ii) Is the order in which you play them important?

(i) Choice of suits: Clearly you must go for clubs and diamonds; they will provide five or even six tricks if the king of clubs is right.

(iv) Order of play: Let us recap briefly on the all-important problem at no trumps (both in defence and attack). West has led a suit in which you possess five cards and two winners, and you will have to give up the lead once or twice according to the position of the king of clubs.

What will happen if you begin with the club finesse and it fails?
East will finish setting up his partner's suit, and you will be defeated if West has the ace of diamonds together with the long hearts.

So what is the correct line?
You must begin with the diamonds in order to render West harmless, and take the club finesse later. One of two things will result from this:

(a) It will win and you will make ten tricks.

(b) It will fail but nine tricks are assured because if West has five hearts West he will be unable to regain the lead.

The Full Deal

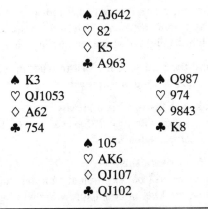

```
              ♠ AJ642
              ♡ 82
              ◇ K5
              ♣ A963
   ♠ K3                    ♠ Q987
   ♡ QJ1053                ♡ 974
   ◇ A62                   ◇ 9843
   ♣ 754                   ♣ K8
              ♠ 105
              ♡ AK6
              ◇ QJ107
              ♣ QJ102
```

Guiding Principle

When you require tricks from two suits and possess two guards in the suit led, you should begin with the suit in which the dangerous opponent has a potential entry.

Deal No. 20

Dealer North. Game All.

♠ AQ
♡ J52
◇ 108642
♣ K76

♠ 6532
♡ AQ104
◇ AK
♣ A85

Lead: ♠J

South	West	North	East
1NT	Pass	3NT	All Pass

How many winners do you have?
1 in spades, 1 in hearts, 2 in diamonds, 2 in clubs = 6 tricks.

You require three more, perhaps only two if the spade finesse succeeds. You therefore put on dummy's queen which East 'naturally' wins with the king, continuing with the eight of spades to dummy's ace.

Where will you find the 3 missing tricks and what must you hope for?
In hearts, provided that the king is with East.

Which heart breaks are favourable and why?
Singleton king, Kx, or Kxx with East. If East has four to the king you will not succeed against correct defence.

How do you handle this suit, then?
If it is divided 3-3 there will be no problem and you can lead dummy's knave, but supposing the king is doubleton, what will happen if you do begin with the knave? Well, East will simply cover and you will be forced to concede the fourth round to West.

What is the solution, then?
You must clearly be thrifty with your honours, since you do have a further entry to the table. Play the two of hearts to the queen. When this holds,

return to dummy with the king of clubs and play another small heart. When East's king appears you will make the four heart tricks which are essential for your contract.

The Full Deal

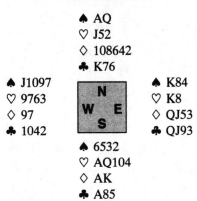

♠ AQ
♡ J52
◇ 108642
♣ K76

♠ J1097   ♠ K84
♡ 9763   ♡ K8
◇ 97   ◇ QJ53
♣ 1042   ♣ QJ93

♠ 6532
♡ AQ104
◇ AK
♣ A85

Guiding Principle

If you have sufficient entries, do not play an honour towards the finesse on either of the first two rounds of the suit with holdings such as:

Qxx   or   Jxx

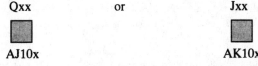

AJ10x   AK10x

... that is to say, whenever you are missing any of the vital intermediates (the nine in the two foregoing examples).

Deal No. 21

Dealer West. North/South Game.

```
          ♠ KQ6
          ♡ 1054
          ◊ J863
          ♣ A83
              N
          W       E
              S
          ♠ AJ3
          ♡ QJ9
          ◊ AQ109
          ♣ K52
```

Lead: ♡6

South	West	North	East
–	Pass	Pass	Pass
1NT	Pass	3NT	All Pass

Firstly, count your certain tricks.
3 in spades, 1 in hearts (after the obvious continuation), 1 in diamonds, 2 in clubs = 7 tricks. You need two more.

Where will you look for the missing tricks?
In diamonds, obviously. If East has the king (50 per cent) you will make ten tricks.

However, there is danger just around the corner. What is it?
West has led a heart, a suit in which you are weak. If the hearts are 4-3 (62 per cent), East/West will take only three or four tricks (three hearts and possibly a diamond), but if they are 5-2, and the length presumably with West as the lead shows, then you are risking the loss of four heart tricks and the king of diamonds.

On the lead of the six of hearts, East plays the king and returns the two. West covers your queen with the ace and continues at Trick 3 with the three of hearts on which East discards the four of spades.

How are the hearts divided?
Alas 5-2, and West has two tricks all ready to cash.

You cross to dummy with a spade and put into operation your initial plan to establish the diamonds.

Which diamond do you play from dummy?
The knave. If East possesses the king he may well observe the rule of covering an honour with an honour thus saving you any further worry. Perhaps he doesn't feel like making things easy for you since he contributes the two of diamonds without turning a hair.

What do you play from your hand?
Remember that West is the dangerous opponent for he has enough established hearts to defeat you. If he also has the king of diamonds you will not make the contract unless …? the king is singleton, so go up with your ace and enjoy West's discomfiture when he reluctantly drops the bare king.

Can your play of the ace endanger the contract of 3NT?
In no way, since your prime objective is to make nine tricks and should the king of diamonds be with East you will give up a trick to him, thereby establishing the two tricks you require for your contract. East will have no way of reaching his partner. Should West have had the king of diamonds guarded there was no way of making the contract.

The Full Deal

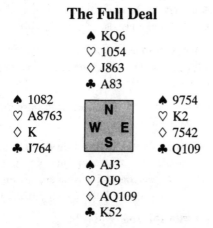

```
              ♠ KQ6
              ♡ 1054
              ◇ J863
              ♣ A83
  ♠ 1082                    ♠ 9754
  ♡ A8763        N          ♡ K2
  ◇ K         W     E       ◇ 7542
  ♣ J764         S          ♣ Q109
              ♠ AJ3
              ♡ QJ9
              ◇ AQ109
              ♣ K52
```

Guiding Principle

If one of your opponents is dangerous you must take all necessary precautions to avoid giving him the lead. One of these is the rejection of a finesse.

Deal No. 22

Dealer East. North/South Game

♠ J754
♡ K96
◇ KJ2
♣ K32

♠ A63
♡ A8
◇ A9754
♣ A106

Lead: ♡Q

South	West	North	East
–	–	–	Pass
1NT	Pass	3NT	All Pass

How many immediate tricks do you have?
1 in spades, 2 in hearts, 2 in diamonds, 2 in clubs = 7 tricks.

How will you establish two extra tricks?
Obviously in diamonds, since your two hands contain eight cards and you are missing only the queen and the ten.

Is it essential for you to capture the queen of diamonds?
Indeed no, only two extra tricks are required.

In such a case, then, what should you be thinking about?
A safety-play, and in this case a text-book one: you must abandon the usual handling of the suit consisting of finessing against the queen in order to assure four tricks against any distribution, even Q10xx with East.

Are you conversant with this safety-play?
You must first cash the honour accompanying the knave, then after re-entering your hand, play small towards Jx. Either:

(i)   West has Q10xx in which case the knave will win the trick.

(ii) East has Q10xx in which case the knave will force the queen and the ten will later be captured by finesse.

Is there any necessity for ducking the opening lead?
No, for you do not intend to give up the lead more than once, and a spade switch at Trick 2 might prove disastrous. Therefore, Trick 1: ace of hearts, Trick 2: diamond to the king, Trick 3: club to the ace followed by a small diamond towards Jx. West discards a spade. Then back to dummy to play the two of diamonds which will allow you to capture East's remaining 106.

The Full Deal

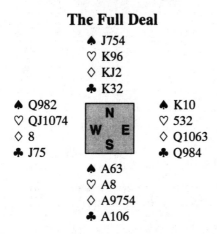

```
              ♠ J754
              ♡ K96
              ◇ KJ2
              ♣ K32
  ♠ Q982        N        ♠ K10
  ♡ QJ1074   W     E     ♡ 532
  ◇ 8           S        ◇ Q1063
  ♣ J75                  ♣ Q984
              ♠ A63
              ♡ A8
              ◇ A9754
              ♣ A106
```

Guiding Principle

Whenever your contract appears to be in no danger, adopt the most pessimistic outlook. Take out insurance by visualising the worst possible distributions and take the safety-play which is appropriate to the occasion. Always be willing to abandon one trick for the sake of not losing more:

KJx

A9xxx

Play the king first, then small towards the knave.

AJxx   or   AJxxx

K9xx   K9x

Play the ace first, then small towards K9. Play the 9 if East follows.

Deal No. 23

Dealer South. Love All.

♠ J85
♡ Q42
◇ KJ63
♣ Q83

♠ A63
♡ 97
◇ AQ5
♣ AK642

Lead: ♣J. East plays the seven

South	West	North	East
1NT	Pass	3NT	All Pass

How many certain winners?

1 in spades, 4 in diamonds, 3 in clubs = 8 tricks.

Is there any glimmer of a ninth?

In hearts and spades the prospects are not promising, and if you broach either of these yourself you will be running the risk of immediate defeat. Only the club suit remains. If the clubs are 3-2 you will have five running club tricks but West probably has four since he has led the suit.

If you win the first club and continue the suit, what will happen?

East will discard and doubtless give his partner a heart signal. You will lose a club and four or five hearts, for it is unlikely that West has both ace and king of this latter suit. You must therefore duck the knave of clubs as though you feared the suit.

Is it possible to cause West to go wrong (without being unethical, of course)?

When faced with situations like these, you should apply a simple but efficient technique against defenders who observe and interpret the small cards furnished by their partner. As declarer, you should make a habit of selecting the card which you yourself would play if you were defending: you signal if you wish partner to continue the suit, and discourage if not.

In the present example you choose the four or the six of clubs. On seeing his partner's seven West will doubtless interpret this as an encouraging signal, and noting that the two is missing he will see no reason for changing his tack. Put yourself in his place: he remains on lead with the knave of clubs; what card would East play if he held ♣AK72? ... the seven, wouldn't he?

West will persist with another club simultaneously discovering the heart signal and his partner's consternation!

The Full Deal

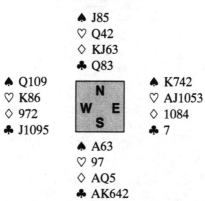

```
              ♠ J85
              ♡ Q42
              ◇ KJ63
              ♣ Q83
  ♠ Q109                      ♠ K742
  ♡ K86          N            ♡ AJ1053
  ◇ 972       W     E         ◇ 1084
  ♣ J1095        S            ♣ 7
              ♠ A63
              ♡ 97
              ◇ AQ5
              ♣ AK642
```

Guiding Principle

A knowledgeable declarer must cultivate the same signalling habits as a defender. There is little doubt that this technique will bring in many valuable points.

Deal No. 24

Dealer South. Love All.

♠ 1073
♡ A65
◇ QJ3
♣ AQ72

♠ A94
♡ Q103
◇ A10982
♣ K5

Lead: ♡2

South	West	North	East
1◇	Pass	2♣	Pass
2NT	Pass	3NT	All Pass

Winner count?
1 in spades, 1 in hearts, 1 in diamonds, 3 in clubs = 6 tricks.

You require three further tricks and you will have no difficulty in finding these in diamonds. If the finesse against the king is successful you will even set up four.

At first sight the contract poses no problems. Furthermore even the lead seems favourable. Nevertheless, you must be on your guard.

If you allow the opening lead to run to your hand and East produces the king, what may happen?
On seeing his partner's two, East will doubtless realise that West has only four hearts, and that this will not be sufficient to defeat your game; with a heart trick in the bag he may now find the dangerous spade switch and you could lose a heart, three spades and the king of diamonds.

How will you avoid this pitfall?
At bridge too, greed is a reprehensible failing, and you should call for dummy's ace of hearts. Nothing can endanger your contract now, since you will play a diamond immediately and if West has the king, your queen of hearts will remain protected.

The Full Deal

```
              ♠ 1073
              ♡ A65
              ◇ QJ3
              ♣ AQ72
♠ J862                        ♠ KQ5
♡ J972         N              ♡ K84
◇ K74        W   E            ◇ 65
♣ 106          S              ♣ J9843
              ♠ A94
              ♡ Q103
              ◇ A10982
              ♣ K5
```

Guiding Principle

At teams or rubber bridge the understandable desire to realise the maximum number of tricks should never induce you to put the success of your contract at risk. Always opt for the 100 per cent line if there is one.

Deal No. 25

Dealer North. East/West Game.

```
              ♠ Q7
              ♡ A95
              ◇ AK954
              ♣ 763

                 N
              W     E
                 S

              ♠ AK5
              ♡ 10832
              ◇ 2
              ♣ A9854
```

Lead: ♠J

South	West	North	East
–	–	1◇	Pass
	Pass	2◇	Pass
2NT	Pass	3NT	All Pass

How many top tricks do you have?

3 in spades, 1 in hearts, 2 in diamonds, 1 in clubs = 7 tricks.

Where do you expect to find the two missing tricks?

Even if there is a favourable 4-3 diamond break, that suit can only provide one long trick. On the other hand you have eight clubs between your two hands which will provide two extra tricks on a 3-2 break.

How many times will you have to give up the lead?

Twice. Now then, you have three stoppers in spades and two in diamonds. In hearts, your combined holding makes it impossible for the opponents to cash more than two tricks in the suit, and you are therefore under no threat in the race for suit-establishment.

Do you have sufficient entries?

At first glance yes, thanks to the ace and king of spades. However, if you began establishing the club suit by playing the ace you would be running the risk of losing not only your two long card tricks, but also the ace of spades if the defenders refused to play a third round of the suit.

What is the answer, then?
Duck twice in clubs in order to preserve an entry to your hand.

Trick 1: queen of spades, Trick 2: low club from both hands, Trick 3: ten of spades from West to your ace, Trick 4: low club from both hands again (East and West following).

There is only one club out now, and even if the defence does not play another round of spades, you will have nine tricks whatever they choose to switch to, and these will be made up of three spades, one heart, two diamonds and three clubs.

The Full Deal

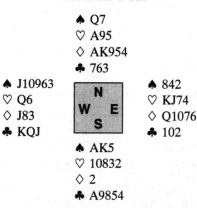

```
                    ♠ Q7
                    ♡ A95
                    ◇ AK954
                    ♣ 763
    ♠ J10963           N          ♠ 842
    ♡ Q6          W         E      ♡ KJ74
    ◇ J83              S          ◇ Q1076
    ♣ KQJ                         ♣ 102
                    ♠ AK5
                    ♡ 10832
                    ◇ 2
                    ♣ A9854
```

Guiding Principle

As a general rule, you should apply the ducking principle whenever the hand with length in the suit is lacking in entries.

Deal No. 26

Dealer East. Game All.

♠ 8754
♥ AQ
♦ K6532
♣ Q3

♠ A63
♥ K7
♦ A84
♣ AJ652

Lead: ♦Q. East discards the ♥2

South	West	North	East
–	–	–	Pass
1NT	Pass	3NT	All Pass

How many tricks on top?
1 in spades, 2 in hearts, 2 in diamonds, 1 in clubs = 6 certain tricks.

Without the lead, revealing East's void, you would have sought to establish two long diamonds (3-2 break, 68 per cent), and the club suit would have provided the ninth trick. As it is, your diamonds have turned out to be dangerous and you will have to bank on the club suit.

Do you know the correct technique with suits like: AQxxx opposite Jx or AJxxx opposite Qx?
In any event you can never make five tricks even if the finesse succeeds, for there are no intermediates.

How should you set about it, then?
You must play towards the doubleton honour (Jx or Qx).

Why?
If West has the doubleton king he will have to play it immediately and you will make four tricks. This will work also, of course, if the suit is 3-3.

The Full Deal

```
              ♠ 8754
              ♡ AQ
              ◇ K6532
              ♣ Q3
  ♠ J2                        ♠ KQ109
  ♡ 10943        N            ♡ J8652
  ◇ QJ1097   W     E          ◇ –
  ♣ K8           S            ♣ 10974
              ♠ A63
              ♡ K7
              ◇ A84
              ♣ AJ652
```

Guiding Principle

Experienced players are aware of and apply the technique required for the most common suit combinations. While this aspect of bridge may seem somewhat dry, any efforts which you bring to bear in this field will certainly prove profitable.

Deal No. 27

Dealer West. Love All.

　　　　　　♠ KQ65
　　　　　　♡ 83
　　　　　　◇ K7
　　　　　　♣ AJ1094

　　　　　　♠ A3
　　　　　　♡ K42
　　　　　　◇ A8652
　　　　　　♣ K83

Lead: ♡9

South	West	North	East
–	Pass	1♣	2♡(i)
3♡(ii)	Pass	3♠	Pass
3NT	All Pass		

(i) Mini pre-empt with six or more cards

(ii) This cuebid after partner's minor-suit opening is primarily a demand to bid no trumps with a guard or half guard in the overcaller's suit. It would be preferable for North, holding Jx, Qx, or Jxx, to have the lead run up to him.

Trick total?
3 in spades, 1 in hearts (after the lead), 2 in diamonds, 2 in clubs = 8 tricks. One extra trick will be enough.

From which suit?
Clubs, naturally. If the finesse works, you will make three extra tricks.

At Trick 1, East overtakes the nine of hearts with the ten.

What manoeuvre is East attempting?
He is trying a defensive duck in order to maintain communications with his partner, who according to the bidding has a maximum of two hearts.

Do you take the king or do you duck too?
Resist the temptation to take your heart trick immediately and allow your right-hand opponent to hold the trick (the position of the ace is obvious). If you do take the king of hearts at Trick 1 you will be forced to guess the position of the queen of clubs. You have already realised that it is better to rely on solutions guaranteed by rationalisation than resort to divination, and if you refuse the king of hearts now it will be possible to ensure your contract.

Do you see how?
When you play the club suit you will proceed in such a way as to prevent East from gaining the lead. It will not matter if West can win the queen of clubs since he will no longer have a heart to play.

East continues with ace and another heart. You take your king while West and dummy discard spades.

What now?
Cross to dummy with the king of diamonds and play the knave of clubs which you run and which holds the trick. Continue with the four of clubs to your eight, West discarding, then cash the king. You will thus come to eleven tricks with no danger.

The Full Deal

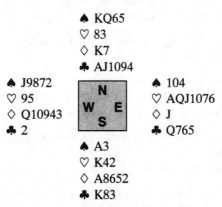

```
              ♠ KQ65
              ♡ 83
              ◇ K7
              ♣ AJ1094
 ♠ J9872        N        ♠ 104
 ♡ 95      W         E   ♡ AQJ1076
 ◇ Q10943       S        ◇ J
 ♣ 2                     ♣ Q765
              ♠ A3
              ♡ K42
              ◇ A8652
              ♣ K83
```

Guiding Principle

Duck according to the bidding, and orientate your finesses so as to avoid giving the lead to the dangerous opponent.

Deal No. 28

Dealer South. North/South Game.

♠ 64
♡ A63
◇ 1082
♣ AK1062

♠ KJ8
♡ K854
◇ AK7
♣ J94

Lead: ♠7. East plays the nine

South	West	North	East
1♡	1♠	2♣	Pass
2NT	Pass	3NT	All Pass

What do you infer from the bidding and the lead?

West possesses at least five spades, and the Rule of 11 tells you that East has one card higher than the seven. Before proceeding, count your sure tricks:

1 in spades (after the lead), 2 in hearts, 2 in diamonds, 2 in clubs = 7 tricks, and two more are required.

Which suit will provide these?

The clubs. You hold AK10xx opposite J9x and when the queen has appeared, the two or three extra tricks will be yours.

East having played the nine of spades at Trick 1, what cards does West have in his suit?

AQ107x, the fifth card not being known.

Obviously you are forced to win the first trick with the knave of spades and you set about establishing the clubs.

How precisely?

The normal way is to test the suit by laying down the ace in order to guard against a singleton queen with East, and then return to hand in order to finesse against West.

But will you play like this?
Think now: you still have a spade guard in your hand, but only on condition that East does not gain the lead.

So how will you play the clubs?
Cash the ace and king and if you are lucky enough to drop the doubleton queen from East you can congratulate yourself on the accuracy of your analysis.

If the queen does not fall, what must you hope for?
That it is West who has it: certainly you will have sacrificed a trick, but remember that four club tricks are enough, and as West has no means of putting his partner in you will have brought home the contract.

(It must be pointed out that if East had the guarded queen of clubs, there is no way of making the contract but you would have played correctly.)

The Full Deal

```
            ♠ 64
            ♡ A63
            ◇ 1082
            ♣ AK1062
♠ AQ1072                    ♠ 953
♡ Q2           N            ♡ J1097
◇ Q63       W     E         ◇ J954
♣ 753          S            ♣ Q8
            ♠ KJ8
            ♡ K854
            ◇ AK7
            ♣ J94
```

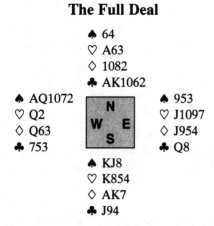

Guiding Principle

When one of your opponents is dangerous, you must frequently be prepared to depart from normal practice in the handling of the suit to be established in order to prevent him from gaining the lead. The rejection of a finesse will sometimes cost a trick but will increase the probability of success of your contract, and at rubber bridge or teams it is essential.

Deal No. 29

Dealer North. Game All.

♠ 65
♡ KQJ85
◇ 98
♣ Q1082

```
      N
   W     E
      S
```

♠ AKJ4
♡ 109
◇ AQ52
♣ AJ9

Lead: ♣5

South	West	North	East
–	–	Pass	Pass
1◇	Pass	1♡	Pass
2NT	Pass	3♣	Pass
3NT	All Pass		

How many sure tricks do you have?
2 in spades, 1 in diamonds, 2 in clubs (after the lead) = 5 tricks. You need to establish four tricks and clearly the heart suit will provide them. However, there is danger threatening.

What is it?
The opponent holding the ace of hearts will hold up in order to cut your communications with dummy.

But can you not be certain of reaching the table? How?
Yes, in clubs, provided you play neither the ten or the queen from dummy at Trick 1 and win with the ace!

Why?
You will remain with J9 in hand opposite Q108 and nothing will be able to prevent you from reaching the dummy.

You therefore win the ace of clubs and continue with the ten of hearts, followed by the nine, not forgetting to overtake with dummy's knave.

East takes with the ace of hearts and returns the knave of diamonds. Do you finesse against the king?
Certainly not, for if it fails you could lose three tricks in diamonds, the ace of hearts and the king of clubs. Remember that two diamond tricks are not essential for success. You go up with the ace of diamonds and continue with the knave of clubs.

Why do you not fear the king of clubs with East?
The Rule of 11 has revealed all: the five of clubs plus six higher ranking cards, all of which are visible to you. East will not regain the lead and the queen of diamonds is therefore protected.

Which card do you play on the knave of clubs?
The queen, then cash three heart winners. You will thus make two spades, four hearts, one diamond and two clubs.

Why did West not play the king of clubs on your knave?
He would have been giving you an extra trick?

The Full Deal

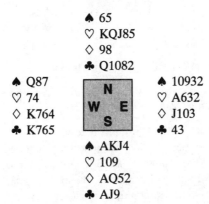

```
              ♠ 65
              ♡ KQJ85
              ◇ 98
              ♣ Q1082
 ♠ Q87                      ♠ 10932
 ♡ 74          N            ♡ A632
 ◇ K764      W   E          ◇ J103
 ♣ K765        S            ♣ 43
              ♠ AKJ4
              ♡ 109
              ◇ AQ52
              ♣ AJ9
```

Guiding Principle

Take good care to preserve your communications with the hand containing a suit which can be established. If need be win a trick with an unnecessarily high card.

Deal No. 30

Dealer South. Game All.

♠ K83
♡ KQ63
◇ A5
♣ K872

♠ AQ9
♡ J2
◇ 10973
♣ AQ65

Lead: ◇6

South	West	North	East
1♣	Pass	1♡	Pass
1NT	Pass	3NT	All Pass

Sure trick total?
3 in spades, 1 in diamonds, 3 in clubs = 7 tricks.

The two missing tricks are easy to find: with KQxx opposite Jx in hearts you have only to knock out the ace;

Are you worried about the lead, and if so why?
If the suit breaks 4-3 you will lose at most three diamonds and the ace of hearts. However if the diamonds are 5-2, it would appear that you will only be successful if the hand containing the long diamonds does not have the ace of hearts as well. The solution which immediately springs to mind is to duck the opening lead.

Yet, is there no answer if West has both the ace of hearts and five diamonds?
To answer this question ask yourself first of all how many cards higher than the six East holds. One only (11-6 = 5 and you can see four of them).

Next try to picture West's precise diamond holding:
He cannot have KQJ6x otherwise he would have led the king. He has therefore led from a suit containing two honours and you can credit

East with a doubleton honour. In the dangerous case where the diamonds are 5-2, three possible combinations exist: QJ86x opposite Kx; KJ86x opposite Qx or KQ86x opposite Jx.

Have these deductions put you on the right road?
You must block the enemy suit by going up with the ace of diamonds at Trick 1 even if this manoeuvre appears contrary to normal reflexes.

If East plays small he will later be on lead with his honour and unable to continue the suit, and if he chooses to unblock his honour card you will retain a second guard with 109x against West's KJxx. Whatever East decides to do you will make your contract, and if the diamonds do turn out to be ~3 your ploy will have cost nothing.

The Full Deal

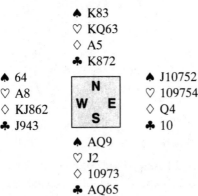

```
              ♠ K83
              ♡ KQ63
              ◇ A5
              ♣ K872
♠ 64                        ♠ J10752
♡ A8          N             ♡ 109754
◇ KJ862    W     E          ◇ Q4
♣ J943        S             ♣ 10
              ♠ AQ9
              ♡ J2
              ◇ 10973
              ♣ AQ65
```

Guiding Principle

One of the weapons available to declarer at no trumps is the blocking of the enemy suit. Consider the following holdings:

A10   or   AJ

9xxx   10xxx

If your left-hand opponent leads the seven go up with the ace immediately.

Deal No. 31

Dealer South. East/West Game.

```
              ♠ 87
              ♡ QJ104
              ◊ A632
              ♣ 765

              N
            W   E
              S

              ♠ AK54
              ♡ 2
              ◊ KQ94
              ♣ AK43
```

Lead: ♣10

South	West	North	East
1◊	Pass	1♡	Pass
1♠	Pass	2◊	Pass
3NT	All Pass		

How many sure tricks do you have?
2 in spades, 3 (or 4) in diamonds, 2 in clubs = 7 tricks.

Where will the two missing tricks come from?
The spade suit holds no hope; the eighth trick will come from diamonds if the suit divides 3-2 (68 per cent); in clubs you could set up a long card if the suit breaks 3-3 (38 per cent); however, West has led the ten, which could be from a doubleton or from length, and it is likely that this suit will break 4-2. In hearts you have QJ10, and so the ninth trick will come from that suit. However, you must reflect that communications are very thin.

How many entries are required in dummy?
Two are needed, one to play the second round of hearts and one to reach the established queen. It appears that only one exists: the ace of diamonds.

Can you see a solution? Do you not have a second entry to the table?
Yes, in diamonds, provided that you handle the suit with care. You will attack the suit by laying down the king and then the queen, and if both opponents follow as you hope they will (a necessary hypothesis for the contract to succeed), the remaining diamond layout will be as follows:

A6

94

You will continue with the nine to the ace (first entry) and later the second entry will be furnished by the play of the four of diamonds to dummy's six.

Is it advisable to duck the opening lead?
You might consider ducking the ten of clubs, thus if the opponents persist with the suit you will be able to verify whether or not it is breaking 3-3. But should West decide to abandon the club suit and switch to spades you would lose one club, two hearts and two spades, and you would be defeated. Consequently, take no risks, win the first trick with the ace of clubs and play the two of hearts to dummy's ten. As the full deal shows, the opponents can only take two clubs and two hearts:

The Full Deal

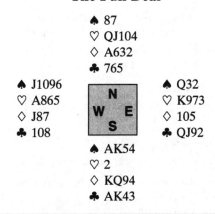

♠ 87
♡ QJ104
♢ A632
♣ 765

♠ J1096   ♠ Q32
♡ A865   ♡ K973
♢ J87   ♢ 105
♣ 108   ♣ QJ92

♠ AK54
♡ 2
♢ KQ94
♣ AK43

Guiding Principle

The handling of a suit in which you possess all the tricks should always be effected with care: always take into consideration those entries which will be required for reaching your established winners in the other suits. For example, holding AKQ4 opposite J652, four entries are possible in the North hand if the outstanding cards are 3-2: play the ace-king to check the distribution, taking care to play the six and five, then the knave to the queen and finally the two to the four.

Deal No. 32

Dealer West. North/South Game.

```
                    ♠ J62
                    ♡ A
                    ◇ QJ43
                    ♣ KQ987
```

```
                    ♠ A1074
                    ♡ KJ3
                    ◇ A2
                    ♣ J1065
```

Lead: ♡6

South	West	North	East
–	Pass	1♣	Pass
1♠	Pass	2♣	Pass
3NT	All Pass		

Count your immediate tricks.
1 in spades, 2 in hearts, 1 in diamonds = 4 tricks. Your objective is to establish five more.

Which suits will provide the tricks?
(i)   The clubs will furnish four tricks with no problems;
(ii) In spades your chances are thin for the knave and ten are divided between your two hands and without the nine you have no genuine finesse position: East would have to possess both honours;
(iii) In diamonds it is possible to set up a trick.

Therefore the clubs and diamonds will provide the extra tricks.

In which order will you tackle these suits?
It is tempting to set about your longest suit first, that is, clubs; however, West's heart attack has left you with only KJ to guard that suit.

What would happen if East should turn up with the ace of clubs?
He would play it immediately and quickly return a heart through your holding. Your knave would lose to the queen and West would lose no time

in establishing his suit. If he has the guarded king of diamonds you will be defeated.

Any declarer with foresight should repress the desire to set up his best suit first and at Trick 2 should lead the queen of diamonds. West can win this trick if he likes but will be unable to continue hearts without playing into your tenace. The clubs can now be set up without danger.

The Full Deal

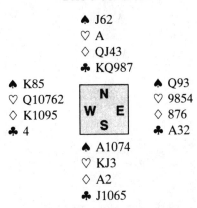

```
                 ♠ J62
                 ♡ A
                 ◇ QJ43
                 ♣ KQ987
  ♠ K85          N          ♠ Q93
  ♡ Q10762    W     E       ♡ 9854
  ◇ K1095        S          ◇ 876
  ♣ 4                       ♣ A32
                 ♠ A1074
                 ♡ KJ3
                 ◇ A2
                 ♣ J1065
```

Guiding Principle

Beginners are normally taught to play on their best suits first, notably those where an ace has to be knocked out in preference to those where a king is missing. This rule, however, is subject to numerous exceptions due to the presence of an opponent who is more dangerous than the other. Thus, as you have just witnessed, it was not only essential to begin with the diamonds but also take an aggressive finesse by leading the queen rather than resort to the text-book handling of cashing the ace first then playing small towards QJx. Two measures were indispensable:

(i) Set up a quick diamond trick;

(ii) Avoid giving East the lead.

Deal No. 33

Dealer South. North/South Game.

♠ Q76
♡ 93
◇ 86
♣ AQ10983

♠ AJ10
♡ AK72
◇ KQ53
♣ J2

Lead: ♠5

South	West	North	East
1NT	Pass	3NT	All Pass

Count your certain tricks.
2 in spades (after the lead), 2 in hearts, 1 in clubs = 5 tricks.

Which suit will provide the extra tricks?
Clubs, of course. You may hope that the king is with West and lead the knave; if it holds, continue with a small one towards the table. If West has the doubleton or trebleton king you will make six tricks in the suit.

Imagine now that East has the king. Clearly, five club tricks will suffice, but is there not a danger?
If East is a good defender. he will not take his king of clubs immediately for it is in his interest to cut your communications with the table. (NB. An excellent defender should hold up even with Kx.)

What does this problem consist of, then?
You will have to be able to reach the dummy?

How will you manage that?
Only one card will allow entry: the queen of spades.

What do you infer from the lead?
East holds no card higher than the five. (Rule of 11: 11-5 = 6 cards higher than the five and all these are visible.)

Which cards (a) from the dummy and (b) from your hand should be played at Trick 1?

(a) The queen of spades should be preserved and you should therefore play small from the table;

(b) Foreseeing the possibility of East holding the king of clubs two or three times guarded, or even king to four with West, it is essential to win the first trick with the ace of spades. if you retain Q7 opposite A10 you will deprive yourself of your entry to dummy, but if you leave yourself with Q7 opposite J10 you will be able to overtake your knave with the queen if West plays small. In any case the defenders will be helpless.

The Full Deal

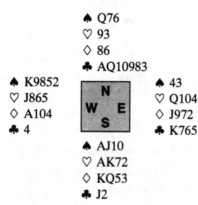

```
                    ♠ Q76
                    ♡ 93
                    ◇ 86
                    ♣ AQ10983
  ♠ K9852                          ♠ 43
  ♡ J865          N                ♡ Q104
  ◇ A104        W   E              ◇ J972
  ♣ 4             S                ♣ K765
                    ♠ AJ10
                    ♡ AK72
                    ◇ KQ53
                    ♣ J2
```

Guiding Principle

Beware of your natural instinct for economy when it is a question of preserving communications.

Deal No. 34

Dealer South. Love All.

♠ A82
♡ K843
◇ 6
♣ AJ954

```
    N
  W   E
    S
```

♠ K75
♡ AQ6
◇ KQ73
♣ Q103

Lead: ◇5

South	West	North	East
1NT	Pass	2♣	Pass
2◇	Pass	3NT	All Pass

Your sure trick count?
2 in spades, 3 in hearts, 1 in diamonds (after the lead), 1 in clubs = 7 tricks.

The club suit will obviously provide the extra tricks. You could even capture king to four with West thanks to your intermediates.

Do you duck the opening lead?
Apply the Rule of 11: 11·5 = 6, which informs us that North, East and South hold six cards higher than the five; as four of these are on view, East has the other two. If one of these is the ace, the contract will present no difficulty.

It is only after these preliminary reflections that you call for dummy's six. The nine appears on your right. Before playing automatically to Trick 1, think about the problem posed.

First of all, to what division of the outstanding cards should you pay particular attention?
The 5-3 break, since should the diamonds prove to be 4-4 you will lose at most four tricks. This first point having been settled, try to visualise precisely East/West's diamond holdings: East has played the nine at Trick 1, therefore his holding must be l09x.

Why?

With 98x he would have played the eight, the lower of two equivalents; with J9x he would have played the knave (the highest), and with A9x, the ace. Consequently if the diamonds are 5-3, West has AJ85x and East 109x.

What will happen if you win the nine of diamonds?

If East has the king of clubs he will return the ten of diamonds and you will not be able to avoid defeat.

So what do you do?

Allow East to hold the nine of diamonds. East now continues with the ten of diamonds as foreseen.

Do you cover?

Once more, no, for if you do it will be West's turn to duck, and he will preserve a tenace position of AJ8 over your Q7, which will be sufficient to beat the contract. You must therefore duck twice, and your opponents will be powerless to realise more than four tricks.

The Full Deal

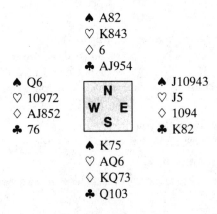

```
                    ♠ A82
                    ♡ K843
                    ◇ 6
                    ♣ AJ954
    ♠ Q6          ┌─────────┐    ♠ J10943
    ♡ 10972       │    N    │    ♡ J5
    ◇ AJ852       │ W     E │    ◇ 1094
    ♣ 76          │    S    │    ♣ K82
                  └─────────┘
                    ♠ K75
                    ♡ AQ6
                    ◇ KQ73
                    ♣ Q103
```

Guiding Principle

Whenever it may be necessary to hold off, only proper rationalisation based on inference from the opening lead (Rule of 11) will guide you towards the winning line.

Deal No. 35

Dealer West. Game All.

> ♠ 72
> ♡ AJ43
> ◇ A98
> ♣ A862

> ♠ A10
> ♡ Q109
> ◇ KJ1054
> ♣ K73

Lead: ♠K

South	West	North	East
–	Pass	1♣	Pass
1◇	1♠	Pass	Pass
3NT	All Pass		

Is there any point in ducking the king of spades?
Hardly, for you have only four cards in spades between your two hands. However, as you do not fear any switch, leave it until the second round. You will cut the communications between your opponents if the spades do turn out to be 7-2.

How many sure tricks do you have?
1 in spades, 1 in hearts, 2 in diamonds, 2 in clubs = 6 tricks.

How will you establish three more?
Either in diamonds, by 'guessing' the position of the queen, or in hearts if the king is with West.

What are the risks?
You cannot afford to make any mistake. One false step (losing finesse) will be punished since both opponents are dangerous in this case. Maybe the gods are 'on your side' now and again, but if they are not so in the present example, it will be in your interest to fall back on proper technique.

What does this consist of?
Whenever you are faced with a crucial choice of finesse, try to combine your chances.

What does this signify in the present case?
Rather than stake everything on one of the two finesses, cash your two top diamonds. If the queen drops your worries are over, and if it does not you fall back on the heart finesse. By playing in this way your chances are much better than 50 per cent: singleton queen (6 per cent) plus doubleton queen (28 per cent) = 34+33 (50 per cent of the remaining chances since that is the odds of the heart king being with West) = 67 per cent.

Recap on the play:
Ace of spades, ace and king of diamonds, and on the second round West plays the queen. You now have nine tricks on top. It costs nothing now to play on West's susceptibilities by banging down the queen of hearts. If he has the king and hasn't yet recovered his composure he will perhaps make the mistake of covering but in any event you put on the ace of hearts in order to cash your well-deserved nine tricks.

The Full Deal

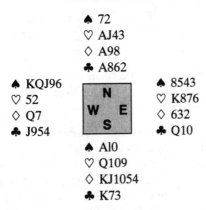

```
                    ♠ 72
                    ♡ AJ43
                    ◇ A98
                    ♣ A862
  ♠ KQJ96                        ♠ 8543
  ♡ 52          N                ♡ K876
  ◇ Q7      W       E            ◇ 632
  ♣ J954        S                ♣ Q10
                    ♠ A10
                    ♡ Q109
                    ◇ KJ1054
                    ♣ K73
```

Guiding Principle

Whenever you are faced with a choice of several finesses without prior information (opponents' bidding or passes are frequent sources of excellent information), ask yourself first of all whether one opponent is more dangerous than the other. It is possible that this important factor will not be present and if such should be the case, you must seek to combine your chances: endeavour to capture a doubleton honour and if this does not work, fall back on a finesse in another suit.

Deal No. 36

Dealer South. Game All.

```
                    ♠ 75
                    ♡ 96
                    ◇ J10986
                    ♣ AK52
                  ┌─────────┐
                  │    N    │
                  │  W   E  │
                  │    S    │
                  └─────────┘
                    ♠ AQ3
                    ♡ Q85
                    ◇ AQ73
                    ♣ Q108
```

Lead: ♠4. East plays the knave

South	West	North	East
1NT	Pass	3NT	All Pass

Count your tricks.

2 in spades (after the lead), 1 in diamonds, 3 in clubs = 6 tricks, and the diamonds will provide three or four more according to the position of the king.

Suppose the diamond finesse fails, what might happen?

West will realise that you still have the spade suit guarded with your ace and from his point of view the only chance of defeating the contract will be to switch to hearts in which case the defence will make at least five tricks (unless East has both the ace and king of hearts).

It is therefore desirable to induce West to continue spades.

How will you manage that?

You must deceive this opponent by winning the opening lead with the ace of spades and n~t the queen. West will be convinced that his partner began with queen-jack and as soon as he comes in with the king of diamonds he will hasten to play another small spade to his partner's presumed queen. Imagine his disappointment when you gather in this trick.

The Full Deal

```
                    ♠ 75
                    ♡ 96
                    ◇ J10986
                    ♣ AK52
  ♠ K10842                        ♠ J96
  ♡ KJ73          ┌─────────┐     ♡ A1042
  ◇ K4            │    N    │     ◇ 52
  ♣ 96            │ W     E │     ♣ J743
                  │    S    │
                  └─────────┘
                    ♠ AQ3
                    ♡ Q85
                    ◇ AQ73
                    ♣ Q108
```

Guiding Principle

Good technique is generally sufficient for giving you the best chance of making your contract, but in certain contexts a well-chosen ruse may be required to come to your aid.

Deal No. 37

Dealer East. North/South Game.

♠ AQJ
♡ K86
◇ 652
♣ K654

♠ K763
♡ AQ54
◇ AQ
♣ AQ2

Lead: ♣J

South	West	North	East
–	–	–	Pass
2NT	Pass	6NT	All Pass

How many tricks can you count?
4 in spades, 3 in hearts, 1 in diamonds, 3 in clubs = 11 tricks.

Where will the twelfth trick come from?
(i)   In hearts or clubs if either suit breaks 3-3.

(ii) The diamond finesse if the king is favourably placed.

How will you begin: finesse or suit-break?
When you have only one trick to find and possess a tenace holding such as
in the diamond suit, always attempt to obtain a count of the adverse distribution, since in the endgame you will frequently be in a position to throw in one
or other of your opponents, and he will then be obliged to open up the crucial
suit himself. Consequently you should delay the finesse until later ....

How will you set about counting the hand?
You cash your winners and as soon as an opponent fails to follow, you will
obtain information which will help you to construct the unseen hands.

Having won the opening lead in your hand, how do you continue?
Cash three rounds of spades, both defenders following three times, then
come to hand with the ace of hearts. On the king of spades which follows
both adversaries throw diamonds, as does dummy. On the third round of

hearts you discover that West began with two only, since he now throws a further diamond. Therefore no twelfth trick from hearts.

You now cash the queen of clubs, then play a small club to dummy's king. On this trick it is East who throws a diamond. So dummy's six of clubs is not good either. However, all is not lost, but ask yourself this question before resorting to the diamond finesse:

How many cards does each opponent have left and what are they?
You have cashed ten tricks and now are now holding the ◇AQ and a losing heart in hand, and dummy holds two small diamonds and a losing club.

How should you continue and why?
The East/West hands are an open book. West began originally with three spades, two hearts, four clubs and consequently four diamonds. East held three spades, four hearts, two clubs and four diamonds. West's remaining cards are two diamonds and a club, and East has two diamonds and a heart.

At this stage the contract is laydown. Just play the six of clubs from the table, throwing the five of hearts from your hand. You will make the last two tricks whoever holds the king of diamonds. You must admit that the 100 per cent line is superior to the one in two chance.

The Full Deal

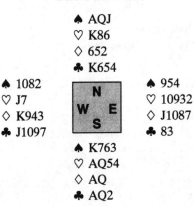

```
                    ♠ AQJ
                    ♡ K86
                    ◇ 652
                    ♣ K654
  ♠ 1082          ┌─────────┐      ♠ 954
  ♡ J7            │    N    │      ♡ 10932
  ◇ K943          │ W     E │      ◇ J1087
  ♣ J1097         │    S    │      ♣ 83
                  └─────────┘
                    ♠ K763
                    ♡ AQ54
                    ◇ AQ
                    ♣ AQ2
```

Guiding Principle

Get yourself into the habit of counting the adverse holdings, and try to visualise the manner in which the play will unfold.

Deal No. 38

Dealer South. Game All.

                    ♠ Q109
                    ♡ A9
                    ◇ AQ83
                    ♣ K954

                    ┌─────────┐
                    │   N   │
                    │ W   E │
                    │   S   │
                    └─────────┘

                    ♠ AJ82
                    ♡ K84
                    ◇ J106
                    ♣ AJ3

Lead: ♡7

South	West	North	East
1♣	Pass	1◇	Pass
1♠	Pass	3♣(i)	Pass
3NT	All Pass		

(i)   Forcing

How many immediate tricks?

1 in spades, 2 in hearts, 1 in diamonds, 2 in clubs = 6 tricks. You have three more to find.

What inference do you draw from the lead? Who is the dangerous opponent?

The seven of hearts cannot be 4th best. As you can already see four cards higher than the seven this would have meant that West had led the seven from QJ107. Had West possessed this holding he would surely have led the queen. The lead is clearly 'top of nothing', and you may reasonably locate QJ10 to any number of hearts on your right. It is therefore East who is the dangerous opponent.

In which suits will you establish your extra tricks?

In spades or in diamonds. Only one of these kings needs to be favourably placed for the contract to succeed, but if the finesse with which you begin fails you will have to try the other one.

Do you duck the opening lead?
Yes, it costs nothing and may be profitable if the hearts break 5-3 or 6-2.

East covers the nine with the ten, thus confirming your initial analysis, and continues with the five to dummy's ace.

Which suit will you play first?
It is essential to attend first of all to the dangerous opponent, that is, East. Since he can only regain the lead in diamonds, begin with that suit. Come to hand with the ace of clubs and run the knave of diamonds. East takes with the king and continues with a heart to your king. You can now cross to the table with a diamond and try the spade finesse. West wins this trick but has no further heart.

The Full Deal

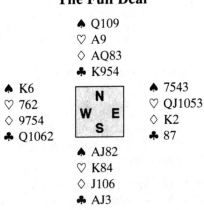

```
                ♠ Q109
                ♡ A9
                ♦ AQ83
                ♣ K954
   ♠ K6           N          ♠ 7543
   ♡ 762       W     E       ♡ QJ1053
   ♦ 9754         S          ♦ K2
   ♣ Q1062                   ♣ 87
                ♠ AJ82
                ♡ K84
                ♦ J106
                ♣ AJ3
```

Guiding Principle

The opening lead can bring vital information, and in the majority of cases will allow declarer to pinpoint the dangerous adversary.

Deal No. 39

Dealer South. Game All.

```
              ♠ K74
              ♡ 7532
              ◇ J54
              ♣ 864
              ┌─────────┐
              │    N    │
              │ W     E │
              │    S    │
              └─────────┘
              ♠ AQJ
              ♡ AK8
              ◇ K92
              ♣ AQJ2
```

Lead: ◇7. East plays the ace

South	West	North	East
2♣	Pass	2◇	Pass
2NT	Pass	3NT	All Pass

How many sure tricks do you have?
3 in spades, 2 in hearts, 1 in diamonds (after the lead), 1 in clubs = 7 certain tricks, and you have to find two more.

What possibilities do you have of realising these extra tricks?
Your best chance with a successful finesse against the king of clubs.

As the cards lie, how many entries to dummy do you have for this finesse?
One only, the king of spades. It will allow the two extra tricks to be established if the king of clubs is well placed, but only if it is doubleton or trebleton. It will not suffice if the king is more than twice guarded.

Are you m a position to overcome this problem?
Yes, since you have the AQJ and the finesse can be repeated. However, in order to repeat the finesse you need a second entry on the table.

Can you see any way of creating one?
The Rule of 11 shows that West's ace of diamonds is the only card higher than the seven in East's hand. The queen is marked with West and therefore the knave is a potential entry.

On what condition?

That you contribute your king of diamonds at Trick 1. This astute unblock will create the extra entry without costing a trick, and you will then be able to finesse twice in clubs instead of once only. The full deal reveals the necessity for this manoeuvre.

The Full Deal

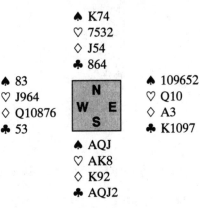

```
                    ♠ K74
                    ♡ 7532
                    ◇ J54
                    ♣ 864
    ♠ 83                        ♠ 109652
    ♡ J964          N           ♡ Q10
    ◇ Q10876    W       E       ◇ A3
    ♣ 53            S           ♣ K1097
                    ♠ AQJ
                    ♡ AK8
                    ◇ K92
                    ♣ AQJ2
```

Guiding Principle

Never yield to an automatic reflex when playing to a trick; always foresee the need to create the maximum number of entries required later for finessing and establishing your suit.

Deal No. 40

Dealer North. North/South Game.

<pre>
                    ♠ Q104
                    ♡ AQ652
                    ◇ AQ5
                    ♣ 108
                   ┌─────────┐
                   │   N   │
                   │ W   E │
                   │   S   │
                   └─────────┘
                    ♠ K82
                    ♡ 43
                    ◇ KJ4
                    ♣ KQJ96
</pre>

Lead: ♠7

South	West	North	East
–	–	1♡	1♠
2♣	Pass	2♡	Pass
3NT	All Pass		

How many certain tricks can you count?

1 in spades (on the lead), 1 in hearts, 3 in diamonds = S tricks. You require four more.

Consider the various possibilities:

(i)   Hearts: even if West has king to three you do not possess enough intermediates to make four tricks;

(ii) Clubs: this suit will provide them easily once the ace has been removed.

However, there is danger close to hand. What is it?

Suppose you play dummy's four on the opening lead: East will put in the nine. If you duck this trick and East has the ace of clubs, he will set up the spades and you will go down in comfort. Similarly if you win with the king and it is West who has the ace of clubs he will continue with a small spade through dummy's Q10 and again East will run enough tricks to defeat you. Perhaps you should put up the ten. No good: East will cover with the knave and wait patiently for West to lead another spade.

Is the problem insoluble, then?
Obviously not, for you have an infallible answer: put up the queen.

You know that East possesses AJ9xx from the lead and the bidding; by selecting the queen you force him to win the trick immediately. If he ducked he would be giving you a second trick in the suit, and your remaining combination of 104 opposite K8 will prevent him from continuing profitably with the suit. He will lose a tempo and you will be ahead in the race for suit-establishment.

The Full Deal

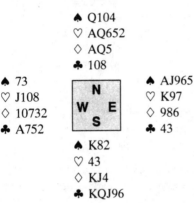

```
              ♠ Q104
              ♡ AQ652
              ◇ AQ5
              ♣ 108
  ♠ 73                      ♠ AJ965
  ♡ J108        N           ♡ K97
  ◇ 10732    W     E        ◇ 986
  ♣ A752        S           ♣ 43
              ♠ K82
              ♡ 43
              ◇ KJ4
              ♣ KQJ96
```

Guiding Principle

Blocking the opponent's suit at Trick 1 may look impressive, but its success depended on finding precisely Q10x in dummy. It is obvious that the contract would have presented no difficulty if played from the correct side. Instead of a premature leap to 3NT South ought to have made a cuebid of two spades, inviting his partner to bid no trumps with a guard or half-guard in the enemy suit. Even Qx alone in the North hand would have been sufficient to ensure two stops with the lead coming from East.

Deal No. 41

Dealer South. Game All.

♠ A63
♡ 64
◇ AQJ8
♣ Q1092

♠ K9
♡ AQ3
◇ 10952
♣ KJ85

Lead: ♡J

South	West	North	East
1♣	Pass	1◇	Pass
1NT	Pass	3NT	All Pass

What is your winner count?
2 in spades, 2 in hearts (after the lead), 1 in diamonds = 5 tricks.

Where will you find four more tricks?
You must establish four winners in the minor suits, since one of these suits alone will not be enough.

In which order will you play those suits?
Since West can only regain the lead in clubs, you must begin with that suit. When an opponent wins the ace of clubs and continues with a heart you can hold up and subsequently take the diamond finesse into the safe hand.

On the knave of hearts East plays the king.

Do you take this trick?
With two guards in the enemy suit and two suits to exploit, the hold-up would normally be correct, but in this example you might well be embarrassed by a defensive switch.

What is it?
The spade switch, for you hold only five cards and two stoppers in that suit. Now then, you would have to give up the lead in clubs and then

possibly lose to the king of diamonds, in which case you would risk the loss of one heart, one club, one diamond and two or three spades.

So win at Trick 1 with the ace of hearts and knock out the ace of clubs. West wins the second round of clubs and continues with the ten of hearts.

What do you do now?
At this stage you must duck absolutely just in case the hearts are 5-3. This manoeuvre costs nothing if they should turn out to be 4-4 after all. You win the third round of hearts, and only now do you take the diamond finesse.

The Full Deal

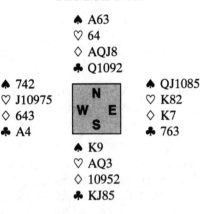

```
              ♠ A63
              ♡ 64
              ◊ AQJ8
              ♣ Q1092
  ♠ 742                      ♠ QJ1085
  ♡ J10975     N             ♡ K82
  ◊ 643      W   E           ◊ K7
  ♣ A4         S             ♣ 763
              ♠ K9
              ♡ AQ3
              ◊ 10952
              ♣ KJ85
```

Guiding Principle

Whenever you have to establish more than one suit and fear a dangerous switch, you may have to win the first round of the enemy suit led and then duck later, if only to cut communications between your adversaries. This technique has been aptly named the 'delayed-duck'.

Deal No. 42

Dealer West. East/West Game.

```
        ♠ 9
        ♡ KQ763
        ◇ AK5
        ♣ KQ93

        N
      W   E
        S

        ♠ AK62
        ♡ J5
        ◇ Q62
        ♣ J1082
```

Lead: ♠Q

South	West	North	East
–	1♠	Dble	Pass
2NT	Pass	3♡	Pass
3NT	All Pass		

Preliminary analysis?
West has opened the bidding and your North/South combined point count is twenty-eight. Therefore West is marked with the outstanding twelve points.

How many tricks do you have?
2 in spades, 3 in diamonds = 5 tricks.

Which suits will provide the required four tricks?
(i)   Hearts, but this suit will only furnish four tricks with a 3-3 break, and remember that this division is only a 36 per cent chance.

(ii) Clubs, but unfortunately only three tricks are possible from this suit and consequently they alone will not suffice for the contract.

It seems reasonable to test the hearts first, but if they are not 3-3, you will lose a tempo in the race for suit-establishment: West will cash his two aces and at least three spades.

But are you not in a position to find the winning line?
The answer to this is that you must win a heart trick without West being
able to capture one of your honour cards, and once this objective has been
achieved, you switch immediately to clubs.

How do you proceed?
Win the opening lead with the king of spades (there is no point in ducking
since you know that West has all the points), and present the five of hearts.
West is helpless: if he goes up with the ace you will make four heart tricks
(unless the ace is singleton), and you will not require a trick from the club
suit; if West plays small, put on the king of hearts and turn your attention
to the club suit.

The Full Deal

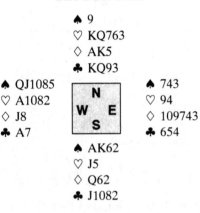

```
              ♠ 9
              ♡ KQ763
              ◇ AK5
              ♣ KQ93
♠ QJ1085                      ♠ 743
♡ A1082      N                ♡ 94
◇ J8       W   E              ◇ 109743
♣ A7         S                ♣ 654
              ♠ AK62
              ♡ J5
              ◇ Q62
              ♣ J1082
```

Guiding Principle

Always take the adverse bidding into account when selecting
your line of play. In this way you may be able to resort to an
unusual manoeuvre which will gain a tempo. This waiting move,
designed to place an opponent on the horns of a dilemma to which
he has no immediate answer, has been named: Morton's Fork.

Deal No. 43

Dealer North. North/South Game.

♠ 93
♡ 7
♢ 862
♣ AKJ9643

```
  N
W   E
  S
```

♠ AKQ7
♡ AKQ
♢ AKQJ
♣ 105

Lead: ♡J

South	West	North	East
–	–	3♣	Pass
4NT	Pass	5◇	Pass
5NT	Pass	6◇	Pass
7NT	All Pass		

Top tricks?
3 in spades, 3 in hearts, 4 in diamonds, 2 in clubs = 12 tricks.

On what will the success of this grand slam depend?
In clubs you have nine cards missing the queen. You can either drop the queen by playing out your top clubs, or take a finesse against West.

What probabilities should guide you towards the correct line?
Cashing the ace and king, since there is a greater chance that the queen will be doubleton than trebleton.

When faced with a dilemma like this, have you no recourse to any other technique? What is it?
Yes; a count of the hand. You cash your top winners in the side suits, hoping to gain valuable information about the adverse distribution.

Win the opening lead with the ace of hearts and cash the ace of clubs. West plays the two and East the eight. Had East shown out, you would have been able to claim.

You now come to hand with the ace of diamonds and play out your winners, keeping a close watch on the cards thrown by your opponents:

(a) Both follow to two more rounds of hearts.

(b) West follows to two rounds of diamonds and then discards a heart.

(c) West follows to two rounds of spades, and discards a heart on the queen.

So, what are the two hands?
East's hand is an open book: he has five spades, three hearts, four diamonds and you have already seen one club. Consequently, the club finesse against West is marked.

The Full Deal

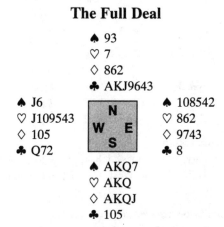

```
                ♠ 93
                ♡ 7
                ◇ 862
                ♣ AKJ9643
  ♠ J6            N          ♠ 108542
  ♡ J109543    W     E       ♡ 862
  ◇ 105           S          ◇ 9743
  ♣ Q72                      ♣ 8
                ♠ AKQ7
                ♡ AKQ
                ◇ AKQJ
                ♣ 105
```

Guiding Principle

Whenever you are faced with a crucial choice between a finesse or suit-break, do not fail to try to count your opponents' hands first: they will be forced to discard while you are running your winners, and your final decision will be taken at a time when you are sure of doing the right thing.

Deal No. 44

Dealer South. Game All.

♠ QJ4
♡ K7
◇ J10853
♣ 852

♠ A62
♡ AQ10
◇ Q962
♣ AQJ

Lead: ♠8

South	West	North	East
1♣	Pass	1◇	1♠
2NT	Pass	3NT	All Pass

Preliminary consideration?
East has bid one spade, a suit in which he doubtless holds at least five cards headed by K109, since West has led the eight (doubleton or singleton).

How many immediate winners do you have?
2 in spades (after the lead), 3 in hearts, 1 in clubs = 6 tricks.

Where do you expect to find the three missing tricks?
The club finesse is insufficient on its own, and you will have to find a trick from the diamond suit.

How many stoppers do you have in spades?
Two only. Now you have to knock out both the ace and king of diamonds and if both these honours are with East you will be defeated.

What must you assume, then?
That West holds at least one of them, since this hypothesis is essential for your success, and that he cannot continue with a spade to help establish his partner's suit. Suppose you instinctively put up one of dummy's honours on the opening lead.

If East covers with the king, what will you do?
You will duck. East will continue spades, and on winning this trick you will be able to set up your diamonds without interference. West will not have a spade to return and the defence will be helpless after your duck at Trick 1. This would seem to be the correct line of play. However, what if you are playing against a defender who doesn't automatically contribute 'the card nearest his thumb' either?

What will he do?
He will refuse to cover the queen of spades, retaining a tenace position over dummy. As soon as you embark on the diamond suit West will rush in with his honour in order to preserve his partner's entry, and shoot back his second spade. Against this defence you will go down in comfort. So the apparently normal ploy of contributing one of dummy's honours at Trick 1 is unsatisfactory.

Is there any way out?
Of course: just play a small spade from both hands. West will continue spades but will not have a further one to play when he comes in with his diamond.

The Full Deal

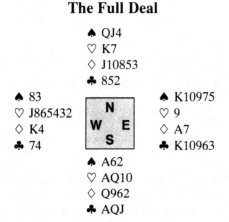

```
                  ♠ QJ4
                  ♡ K7
                  ◇ J10853
                  ♣ 852
    ♠ 83                        ♠ K10975
    ♡ J865432      N            ♡ 9
    ◇ K4        W     E         ◇ A7
    ♣ 74           S            ♣ K10963
                  ♠ A62
                  ♡ AQ10
                  ◇ Q962
                  ♣ AQJ
```

Guiding Principle

Before playing hastily to the first trick, always consider carefully the manner in which the play is likely to unfold. Overcalls provide information from which defenders should not be the only ones to benefit.

Deal No. 45

Dealer South. Love All.

♠ AK85
♡ 654
◇ 954
♣ AQ8

♠ 76
♡ A109
◇ AK632
♣ K75

Lead: ♡3

South	West	North	East
1◇	1♡	1♠	Pass
1NT	Pass	3NT	All Pass

Sure trick count?
2 spades, 1 heart, 2 diamonds and 3 clubs = 8 tricks. One more is needed.

Do you duck the opening lead? How many times?
Naturally, and taking account the Rule of 7, only duck once.

In which suit will you set up your extra trick?
The only chance lies in the diamond suit. If it breaks 3-2 (68 per cent) two long cards can be established.

But what condition will be required for you to succeed?
East will have to hold the three diamonds; in this way West, the dangerous opponent will be unable to regain the lead. Therefore after the initial duck at Trick 1 it would appear sufficient to cash the ace and king of diamonds in the hope that West has the doubleton.

Nevertheless, is there not a winning position when East has two diamonds and West three?
Yes, but then East would have to possess the queen doubleton precisely. By playing twice towards your ace and king you would ensure the success of your contract by avoidance play.

You therefore duck the opening heart lead once only. After winning the heart continuation, cross to the table with a club and play a diamond towards your hand. (If you began with a top diamond from your hand East might well unblock the queen.) On the first round East plays the seven.

And you?
The ace.

How do you continue?
Cross to another club and play another diamond. This time East produces the queen.

Well?
Leave East in possession of this trick and your contract is assured.

The Full Deal

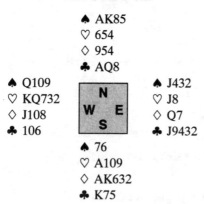

```
              ♠ AK85
              ♡ 654
              ◇ 954
              ♣ AQ8
♠ Q109                      ♠ J432
♡ KQ732        N            ♡ J8
◇ J108      W     E         ◇ Q7
♣ 106          S            ♣ J9432
              ♠ 76
              ♡ A109
              ◇ AK632
              ♣ K75
```

Guiding Principle

Such pretty avoidance plays frequently enhance the chances of success at no trumps and often too in trump contracts. The capacity to picture adverse distributions and the position of honour cards, and then to play accordingly, is the mark of a good player.

NB. Had you held up the ace of hearts until the third round East could have seized the opportunity to discard the queen of diamonds.

Deal No. 46

Dealer South. East/West Game.

♠ K653
♡ Q9
◇ KJ7
♣ A1043

♠ AQ
♡ AJ10
◇ 109432
♣ K65

Lead: ♡4. East plays the two

South	West	North	East
1◇	Pass	1♠	Pass
1NT	Pass	3NT	All Pass

Certain trick total?
3 in spades, 2 in hearts (after the lead), 2 in clubs = 7 tricks.

Which suit will provide the two missing tricks?
Diamonds, obviously.

How do you normally play such a suit?
You play towards the king-jack in the hope that the queen is favourably placed.

It would therefore seem that you should come to hand with a spade at Trick 2 and play a small diamond towards dummy's tenace, whereupon the contract will depend on the favourable position of the queen. If East has it he will return a heart through your hand and you will have to hope for a 4-4 heart break, losing two diamonds and two hearts. If the hearts are 5-3 you will duck East's heart return and pray for him to have the ace of diamonds as well.

Is there not a line of play offering a high percentage chance of success even though East has the queen of diamonds and West the ace of diamonds and five hearts?

Yes, you must hope that your right-hand opponent will be taken in.

Suppose at Trick 2 you negligently play the seven of diamonds towards the closed hand. East will naturally think that you have the ace and it will be very difficult for him to rush in with the queen, for to do so might well be handing you the contract on a plate.

And what if the queen of diamonds is with West?
No problem, for he cannot harm you with a heart continuation without giving you a further trick in the suit. He will have to switch and you will have all the time you require to knock out the ace of diamonds for three extra tricks, making ten in all.

The Full Deal

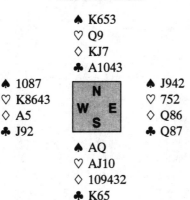

```
              ♠ K653
              ♡ Q9
              ◇ KJ7
              ♣ A1043
♠ 1087                      ♠ J942
♡ K8643        N            ♡ 752
◇ A5        W     E         ◇ Q86
♣ J92          S            ♣ Q87
              ♠ AQ
              ♡ AJ10
              ◇ 109432
              ♣ K65
```

Guiding Principle

You may be frequently forced to resort to unorthodox manoeuvres in order to prevent an opponent from gaining the lead prematurely. If you act quickly, at the beginning of the hand, the defender in question may not have sufficient elements of information to make the right play.

Deal No. 47

Dealer North. North/South Game.

♠ 75
♡ 8543
◇ AKQ42
♣ 63

♠ AK9
♡ A10
◇ 10985
♣ AQ72

Lead: ♡K

South	West	North	East
–	–	Pass	Pass
1NT	Pass	2♣	Pass
2◇	Pass	3NT	All Pass

Immediate trick count?
2 in spades, 1 in hearts, 3 in diamonds, 1 in clubs = 7 tricks.

How do you envisage the success of the contract?
The diamond suit should yield five tricks. You have nine cards between the two hands including the three top honours and only a 4-0 break (9.5 per cent) would appear to cause any difficulty. Should this be the case, your ninth trick could come from a successful club finesse. You ought therefore to make this contract without too much difficulty.

In spite of all these favourable conditions, however, try to uncover the danger which threatens if you do not take care.
In diamonds you possess AKQ42 opposite 10985, and dummy has no outside entry.

What will happen in the event of both 2-2 and 3-1 divisions?
If the diamonds are 2-2 there will be no problem; ace and king first, then small to the ten and back to the two winners on the table. If, on the other hand, an opponent holds ◇Jxx, you will have to play ace, king and queen, and you will then be cut off from the fifth diamond; the suit will be blocked.

Can you see a way of obviating this difficulty?
A first solution which comes to mind is that after discovering that an opponent has ◇Jxx you take advantage of being in the dummy in order to try the club finesse. However, a better chance is to seek to unblock the diamonds yourself, always provided that you are able to throw one of them on another suit. You would then release the fifth diamond without difficulty.

How win you do this?
On the enemy's heart suit, provided that it divides 4-3 or 5-2. When your opponent plays out his master hearts you will get rid of a diamond.

What must you do at Trick 1?
You must duck in order to verify whether East has a second heart. So you allow the king of hearts to hold the trick while East contributes the two. West continues with the queen of hearts which you take, East contributing the seven. Now you cash the ace and king of diamonds to test the suit and West discards a spade on the second round.

How do you continue?
Everything is in place; play the five of hearts from dummy and throw a diamond from your hand. It little matters whether or not West decides to take his two master hearts, since nothing can prevent you from getting at your two long diamonds. The four hands reveal that any other line was doomed to failure.

The Full Deal

```
                ♠ 75
                ♡ 8543
                ◇ AKQ42
                ♣ 63
  ♠ J62                        ♠ Q10843
  ♡ KQJ96        N             ♡ 72
  ◇ 7          W   E           ◇ J63
  ♣ KJ94         S             ♣ 1085
                ♠ AK9
                ♡ A10
                ◇ 10985
                ♣ AQ72
```

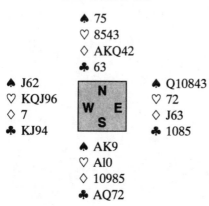

Guiding Principle

Pay careful attention to the potential role of small cards in the suits you intend to develop. Do not allow yourself to be caught unawares by a blockage in your main suit, for such measures as you may have to take must be foreseen at the beginning of the hand.

Had the hearts turned out to be 6-1, the club finesse (after discovering that the diamonds were 3-1) would have constituted your only genuine chance.

Deal No. 48

Dealer East. East/West Game.

♠ AQ54
♥ 63
♦ KQJ6
♣ 542

♠ K62
♥ AKQ10
♦ A53
♣ AJ10

Lead: ♦10

South	West	North	East
–	–	–	Pass
2NT	Pass	3♣(i)	Pass
3♥	Pass	3♠	Pass
3NT	Pass	6NT(ii)	All Pass

(i)   Baron – asking for four-card suits in ascending order

(ii) There cannot be two aces missing (21+12 = 33)

How many sure tricks do you have?
3 in spades, 3 in hearts, 4 in diamonds, 1 in clubs = 11 tricks. One more will bring home the contract.

Review the various options of establishing the extra trick:

(a) In spades, if they break 3-3.

(b) In hearts, by attempting a successful finesse of the ten rather than hoping to bring down the knave in two rounds.

(c) In clubs, if the two missing honours (king and queen) are divided or both with East; simply take two successive finesses.

What are the respective chances of success for each of these manoeuvres?

(a) 3-3 spades break: 36 per cent;

(b) Single finesse: 50 per cent.

(c) A double finesse fails only 25 per cent of the time, i.e. if both the missing honours are unfavourably placed. Consequently its chance of success is 75 per cent.

Therefore except in the case of a clear indication to the contrary (information gleaned from the bidding, for example), select the line of play which offers the maximum chance of success.

Win the opening lead on the table and play the two of clubs to your ten; West wins with the queen and continues with the nine of diamonds which you take with the ace.

How do you continue? Can you attempt to improve your initial chance of 75 per cent? In what way?
At this stage it is possible to keep various extra chances in hand without risk:

(i) You will test the spade suit.

(ii) You will play the hearts from the top without finessing. If the knave falls you will not require a further club finesse.

If the spades break 4-2 and the knave of hearts fails to appear, you will take a further club finesse.

Let us recap on the different phases of the play:
(i) At the very beginning, a small club to the ten and West's queen.

(ii) ♡AKQ, discarding a club from the table, but the knave does not fall.

(iii) King of spades, then ace and queen of spades in order to verify the division; West discards on the third round.

(iv) Three rounds of diamonds, South discarding the ten of hearts on the last one.

(v) Small club towards your AJ. East plays the king which he has been forced to bare, for you have squeezed him! He could not abandon the ten of spades otherwise dummy's five would be high!

The Full Deal

```
              ♠ AQ54
              ♡ 63
              ◇ KQJ6
              ♣ 542
♠ J9          ┌─────────┐      ♠ 10873
♡ J852        │    N    │      ♡ 974
◇ 10987       │ W     E │      ◇ 42
♣ Q93         │    S    │      ♣ K876
              └─────────┘
              ♠ K62
              ♡ AKQ10
              ◇ A53
              ♣ AJ10
```

Guiding Principle

After the opening lead, get yourselves into the habit of evaluating all your chances of success before opting for a particular line of play. In most cases it will be a simple matter of your being aware of basic percentages such as those outlined here.

PART II
GENERAL
REFERENCE SECTION

Suppose you wish to obtain information on a particular aspect: simply refer to this central section and you will immediately have a reference to the deals which relate to your individual problem.

For the explanatory deals in Part I the reference is a number and for the deals constituted by the exercises in Part III the reference is a letter.

The crucial problem at no trumps: the dangerous opponent.
It is absolutely vital to prevent this adversary from gaining the lead for two main reasons:

(a) He has an established suit: 1-8-12-21-27-38-45-A

(b) Your guard in his partner's suit is exposed to a finesse:
   11-28-34-40-G-J-R

There are various solutions to this problem:
1. The duck
   (a) Classic case: 1-11

   (b) Application of the Rules of 7 and 11:
      1-8-10-11-16-28-33-34-38-39-40 45-F-K-N

   (c) Special cases:

      (i) Bath Coup: 15
      (ii) With KQxx: 34
      (iii) With QJx opposite Axx: 44
      (iv) Delayed-duck: 41
      (v) Deceptive duck: 23-P

NB. You must nevertheless be aware that ducking may be fatal. It may be a question of:

      (vi) Averting a dangerous switch: 18-24
      (vii) Blocking the enemy suit: 30

(viii) Retaining a card of exit for a later throw-in: 42-O

(ix)   Creating a second stopper: 5-40

(x)   Preserving a vulnerable holding: 12

2. Finessing into the correct hand: 27-G-J

3. Rejecting a finesse: 16-21-28-A

4. Avoidance: 45-R

5. Second hand high: 40-D

6. Stealing a tempo: 42

7. Choice of order in suit establishment: 16-19-32-38-Q

Communications problems must not be overlooked:
3-4-14-25-29-31-33-39-47-F-H-I-L-N

Suit establishment and safety-plays: 6-9-17-20-22-26-C-E-I-K

The race for suit-establishment: 2-7-13-B

Combined chances and probabilities: 35-48

Inferences from the bidding and opening lead: 11-38-42-44-B-D-O

Counting the hand: 37-43-M

Throw-in: 37-O

Psychological gambits: 24-36-46-P

In order to cope with the exercises that follow a method is suggested according to your level of ability.

Beginners should progress gradually, not embarking on any question until they have checked the accuracy of their response to the preceding one.

Average players should be capable of reviewing the questions in their totality and solving the problems integrally.

Good players and experts can ask their own questions without taking prior account of those which have been suggested.

PART III
EXERCISES A-R

Exercise A

Dealer North. East/West Game.

```
              ♠ AQ5
              ♡ 432
              ◇ Q9654
              ♣ Q7
```

```
              ♠ K64
              ♡ QJ8
              ◇ AJ102
              ♣ AK3
```

Lead: ♡6. East plays the king

South	West	North	East
–	–	Pass	Pass
1NT	Pass	3NT	All Pass

The opponents play three rounds of hearts, East discarding the two of clubs on the third round. You are in hand with the queen of hearts.

Questions

1. How many certain tricks do you have?

2. How do you give yourself the best chance? What must you hope for in order to bring home the contract?

Answers

1. You possess 3 tricks in spades, 1 in hearts, 1 in diamonds, 3 in clubs = 8 tricks.

2. Above all you must prevent West from gaining the lead, for he has two tricks to cash. The choice is clear: if East has the king of diamonds you are in no danger; if, on the other hand, West has it, then the contract appears doomed unless it is bare. No doubt you have discovered the best line: cross to the table with a spade and lead the queen of diamonds (you never know, East might cover it and it doesn't cost anything). East follows with the three, you go right up with the ace and ... West's king falls. He will doubtless regard you with suspicion in future.

And if the king of diamonds is with East? You will certainly have lost a trick but the contract will be in no danger since East can do you no harm.

The Full Deal

```
              ♠ AQ5
              ♡ 432
              ◇ Q9654
              ♣ Q7
♠ 873                        ♠ J1092
♡ A9765        N             ♡ K10
◇ K         W     E          ◇ 873
♣ 10654        S             ♣ J982
              ♠ K64
              ♡ QJ8
              ◇ AJ102
              ♣ AK3
```

NB. You may be in trouble against an expert West. Seeing his partner's king of hearts at Trick 1, West will realise that East cannot possibly have another entry, and when South covers the ten of hearts at Trick 2 West will duck, playing the seven. If you visualise the adverse hearts to be West: A976 and East: K105, you may think that you have no reason for not taking the diamond finesse, since you would expect to lose only a diamond and three hearts. If you suspect West of being capable of such deception you should refuse to be taken in and still play the ace of diamonds, since if you do assume the hearts to be 4-3 it may still only cost one trick, but not the contract, to refuse the finesse. *(Translator's note)*

Exercise B

Dealer East. East/West Game.

> ♠ KQ6
> ♡ 43
> ◇ Q83
> ♣ A6542

> ♠ AJ103
> ♡ A109
> ◇ K102
> ♣ K97

Lead: ♡2

South	West	North	East
–	–	–	Pass
1NT	Pass	3NT	All Pass

East plays the king of hearts at Trick 1 and, if you decide to duck, he will return the five.

Questions

1. Immediate trick total?

2. What inference do you draw from the lead, and do you duck?

3. Where will you find the extra tricks? (As always you must take the defence's tricks into consideration.)

Answers

1. You have 7 sure tricks: 4 in spades, 1 in hearts, 2 in clubs.

2. The hearts are most probably 4-4. Certainly, West may have false-carded on the opening lead, but East played back the five, which would be his lowest of three remaining cards.

   Since you do not fear any switch (in fact you would rather like it), duck twice.

3. At first sight it would seem appropriate to play for a 3-2 club break (68 per cent), but if you have taken the precaution of counting the tricks against you, you will find that they come to five: three hearts, one diamond, and a club voluntarily conceded. This line of play being therefore doomed to failure, you must seek to develop two diamond tricks by playing East for the knave (50 per cent). At Trick 4 play the two of diamonds to the queen which holds (it does not matter where the ace is), and continue with the three towards your hand. You are lucky and West has to play the ace. Your contract is made with four spades, one heart, two diamonds and two clubs.

The Full Deal

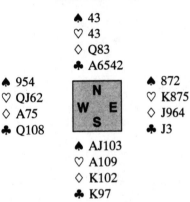

```
                    ♠ 43
                    ♡ 43
                    ◇ Q83
                    ♣ A6542
   ♠ 954            ┌───────┐        ♠ 872
   ♡ QJ62          │   N   │        ♡ K875
   ◇ A75           │ W   E │        ◇ J964
   ♣ Q108          │   S   │        ♣ J3
                    └───────┘
                    ♠ AJ103
                    ♡ A109
                    ◇ K102
                    ♣ K97
```

Exercise C

Dealer West. Love All.

♠ J76
♡ A84
◇ QJ543
♣ 62

♠ AQ
♡ K107
◇ A962
♣ A1084

Lead: ♠5

South	West	North	East
–	Pass	Pass	Pass
1NT	Pass	2NT	Pass
3NT	All Pass		

Questions

1. How many top tricks?

2. Which suit should you establish?

3. How will you play it?

Answers

1. 2 in spades, 2 in hearts, 1 in diamonds, 1 in clubs = 6 tricks. You need three more.

2. Diamonds: you have nine cards between the two hands and you turn your immediate attention to these.

3. Remember that you need only three extra tricks and that you still possess a spade stopper. You must therefore think of how to assure four diamond tricks against any adverse distribution. The missing cards are K1087 and you should make a habit of visualising all the cards held by the defenders.

Against any 2-2 or 3-1 division you will have no problem, consequently you should concentrate on the 4-0 break. There is only one way of dealing with the 4-0 division and that is to play the two of diamonds towards the queen. If West has the four diamonds you will lead twice towards dummy and he will be helpless; if it is East who has them he will win with the king and you will later be able to capture through his ten.

The Full Deal

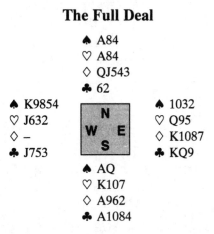

```
                ♠ A84
                ♡ A84
                ◇ QJ543
                ♣ 62
  ♠ K9854                    ♠ 1032
  ♡ J632        N            ♡ Q95
  ◇ -        W     E         ◇ K1087
  ♣ J753        S            ♣ KQ9
                ♠ AQ
                ♡ K107
                ◇ A962
                ♣ A1084
```

There are two contrasting attitudes which all good bridge players should adopt according to circumstances:

(a)   Resolute optimism when faced with a desperate contract: 'I need to find certain cards and distributions in this hand or that and I shall play accordingly'.

(b)   Basic pessimism when confronted by an apparently laydown contract: 'What distribution (even the most outlandish) can endanger my contract? What steps can I reasonably take (without endangering the contract) in order to overcome the potential obstacle? If I can manage to obviate that danger I shall play accordingly.'

Such should be your rationalisation in both these eventualities.

Exercise D

Dealer South. East/West Game.

♠ K104
♡ Q76
◇ AJ107
♣ Q52

♠ Q62
♡ KJ5
◇ KQ9
♣ AJ106

Lead: ♠9

South	West	North	East
1NT	Pass	3NT	All Pass

Questions

1. How many top tricks do you have?

2. What inference do you draw from the lead?

3. Which card do you play from dummy at Trick 1? Why?

4. If you have played correctly at Trick 1, East has had to win; he now returns the nine of clubs; do you finesse? Justify your decision.

5. What tricks will you set up?

Answers

1. You have 6 tricks: 1 in spades (after the lead), 4 in diamonds, 1 in clubs. You require three more.

2. The nine of spades is almost certainly a 'lead for partner', and it would be logical to assume that East is marked with AJxxx.

3. In that case, put up the king of spades at Trick 1. It is a matter of both cutting communications between your opponents and preventing East from returning the suit at no cost to the defence.

4. Since you must prevent West from regaining the lead (he would return another spade before you had knocked out the ace of hearts), you should assume that East's club switch, the nine, would tend to mark West with the king, and should therefore put up the ace.

5. You now proceed to establish a heart trick. East wins the first round; if he returns a spade he will be giving you your ninth trick; he can only put West in with the king of clubs, and this will not harm you since your spade guard is still intact. Your contract will be made with an overtrick: one spade, two hearts, four diamonds and three clubs.

The attentive reader will have noted that the recommended line of play would have failed had the ace of hearts and king of clubs been interchanged, but brilliant or illogical defence has to be accepted from time to time.

Drawing the correct inferences from the cards played by your opponents will enable you to benefit considerably in the long run.

The Full Deal

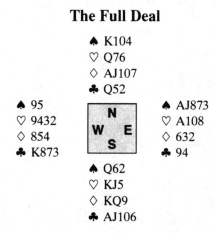

```
              ♠ K104
              ♡ Q76
              ◇ AJ107
              ♣ Q52
  ♠ 95                        ♠ AJ873
  ♡ 9432          N           ♡ A108
  ◇ 854       W     E         ◇ 632
  ♣ K873          S           ♣ 94
              ♠ Q62
              ♡ KJ5
              ◇ KQ9
              ♣ AJ106
```

Exercise E

Dealer South. North/South Game.

- ♠ AK3
- ♡ AQ5
- ◇ J102
- ♣ AK64

- ♠ Q109
- ♡ KJ10
- ◇ AK854
- ♣ 87

Lead: ♡9

South	West	North	East
1NT	Pass	6NT	All Pass

Questions

1. How many top tricks?

2. Only one suit can be established; what distribution do you have to consider?

3. Suppose your partner had bid seven no trumps, how would you play the diamonds?

Answers

1. You can count 3 in spades, 3 in hearts, 2 in diamonds, 2 in clubs = 10 tricks, and you require two more.

2. Only the diamond suit is viable. If you play the ace, then small towards J10 no 3-2 or 4-1 break can worry you, therefore your only consideration should be if one opponent holds all five outstanding diamonds: Q9763. Even though this distribution is extremely rare, you must not overlook the safety play for four tricks which is 100 per cent.

3. In order to guard against 5-0 with either opponent, just play a small
   diamond towards J102: if West discards, East's nine will later be
   picked up by finesse, and if East discards, West not taking his queen
   on the first round, simply return to hand in another suit and lead
   another low diamond to dummy.

The Full Deal

```
              ♠ AQ5
              ♡ J102
              ◇ AK64
              ♣ AK64
♠ J62                          ♠ 8754
♡ 9874          N              ♡ 632
◇ Q9763     W       E          ◇ –
♣ Q             S              ♣ J109532
              ♠ Q109
              ♡ KJ10
              ◇ AK854
              ♣ 87
```

In seven no trumps the safety-play is out of the question; five diamond
tricks are required and you must play accordingly: East must have the
queen either doubleton or two or three times guarded. You must take a first
round finesse by running the knave. You must not test the suit by laying
down the ace for East is more likely to have the queen to four than West
the queen singleton.

This contract has a probability of success of around 45 per cent, which is
not very attractive since a grand slam should not be bid unless it is better
than about 70 per cent.

Exercise F

Dealer East. East/West Game.

♠ 863
♡ J52
◇ A109
♣ 7654

♠ AQJ4
♡ Q103
◇ KQJ
♣ AK9

Lead: ♡7

South	West	North	East
–	–	–	Pass
2NT	Pass	3NT	All Pass

East wins the heart lead with the ace and returns the suit.

Questions

1. Count your sure tricks.

2. Under what conditions will you succeed?

3. Which card will you play from your hand at Trick

Answers

1. 1 in spades, 1 in hearts (after the lead and continuation), 3 in diamonds, 2 in clubs = 7 tricks.

2. The spade suit offers the best prospects: you can establish two tricks in the suit if East has the king, doubleton or trebleton. Why precisely Kx or Kxx? Quite simply, because there is only one entry in dummy: the ace of diamonds.

   At first sight it appears impossible to repeat the spade finesse and therefore prevail against Kxxx or longer with East; in order to overcome this obstacle it is necessary to play spades a second time from the North hand. How can you manage that?

3. The opening lead (seven of hearts) shows that East has only one card higher, the ace, which he has just played. Throw your queen under this and North's knave of hearts will provide the second entry. Your game will be made provided East has the king of spades however many times guarded, and on condition you pay attention to Trick 1.

The Full Deal

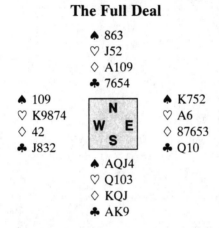

Note that if you retain your queen of hearts in hand at Trick 1 West will always be able to prevent North's knave from becoming an entry.

Exercise G

Dealer West. North/South Game.

♠ 85
♡ KJ102
◇ AJ76
♣ AQJ

```
      N
   W     E
      S
```

♠ KJ10
♡ A9
◇ Q1053
♣ K1094

Lead: ♠7. East plays the six

South	West	North	East
–	2♠(i)	Dble	Pass
3NT	All Pass		

(i)   Weak, 6-10 points

Questions

1. How many top tricks?

2. What is the danger? What suit will you play on?

3. How will you play that suit?

Answers

1. 1 in spades (after the lead), 2 in hearts, 1 in diamonds, 4 in clubs = 8 certain tricks.

2. The weak Two Spade opening and East's six of spades show that the ace and queen are marked with West. West's opening bid showing 6-10 points, he cannot have both the king of diamonds and the queen of hearts. If you take either the diamond or heart finesse against West and it falls, you will be defeated immediately.

Remember, you require only one extra trick, so set up a trick in hearts, taking care not to allow East to gain the lead. Play a heart from the dummy and put in the nine. If West wins with the queen the contract is assured. He will doubtless switch to a diamond, but you will rise with dummy's ace and claim your nine tricks.

3. Recap on the play: ten of spades at Trick 1, club to the queen, two of hearts to your nine which holds. Ace of hearts, small club to the ace (take care not to block the clubs), king of hearts. When the queen of hearts does not appear, overtake the knave of clubs with the king, cash the ten and take your ace of diamonds for nine tricks.

The Full Deal

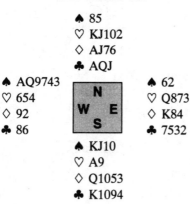

```
                    ♠ 85
                    ♡ KJ102
                    ◇ AJ76
                    ♣ AQJ
    ♠ AQ9743                    ♠ 62
    ♡ 654           N           ♡ Q873
    ◇ 92         W     E        ◇ K84
    ♣ 86            S           ♣ 7532
                    ♠ KJ10
                    ♡ A9
                    ◇ Q1053
                    ♣ K1094
```

Exercise H

Dealer North. North/South Game.

♠ AQ742
♡ KJ10
♢ AK6
♣ K3

	N	
W		E
	S	

♠ 65
♡ A3
♢ 542
♣ QJ10986

Lead: ♡4

South	West	North	East
–	–	1♠	Pass
1NT	Pass	3NT	All Pass

Questions

1. Your winner count?

2. What suit will you establish?

3. What card will you play from dummy at Trick 1? Why?

Answers

1. 1 in spades, 2 in hearts, 2 in diamonds = 5 tricks. You require four more.

2. You will naturally play on clubs. They will furnish five tricks once the ace has gone. Obviously you will begin with the king and continue the suit until the ace appears.

3. At first sight the heart lead seems favourable since you no longer have to guess where the queen is. However, beware! You can bet that a careless declarer will hastily play the ten in order to profit from the free finesse. Well now, what would be the danger in this play? The ten

might be covered by the queen and South can say good-bye to the contract. He will be forced to win with the ace thereby killing the club suit stone dead for lack of a later entry.

Before yielding to his instinct of greed he would have done better to imagine how play would develop, and to this end preserve the only sure entry to his hand: the ace of hearts. Only one card is correct from dummy at Trick 1: the king of hearts (who cares if West has the queen?). The clubs will be established in comfort with the ace of hearts for entry.

You must admit that a goodly number of players do not take time to foresee how the play will go, and of these a large percentage would have defeated themselves in this laydown contract.

The Full Deal

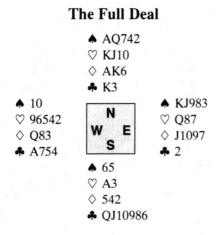

```
              ♠ AQ742
              ♡ KJ10
              ◇ AK6
              ♣ K3
  ♠ 10                        ♠ KJ983
  ♡ 96542       N             ♡ Q87
  ◇ Q83      W     E          ◇ J1097
  ♣ A754        S             ♣ 2
              ♠ 65
              ♡ A3
              ◇ 542
              ♣ QJ10986
```

Exercise I

Dealer South. Love All.

> ♠ 532
> ♡ AQ743
> ◇ 98
> ♣ 764

> ♠ AQ9
> ♡ 82
> ◇ AK62
> ♣ AJ95

Lead: ♠7. East plays the ten

South	West	North	East
1♣	1♠	Pass	Pass
1NT	Pass	3♡	Pass
3NT	All Pass		

Questions

1. How many tricks do you have?

2. What conditions must be present for the contract to succeed?

3. How will you set about the hand?

Answers

1. 2 in spades (after the lead), 1 in hearts, 2 in diamonds, 1 in club = 6 sure tricks.

2. Only one suit is capable of furnishing three extra tricks: hearts. Unfortunately you have only AQxxx opposite two small and no outside entry. In order to establish three tricks the suit must divide 3-3 and the king lie with West. That gives you a mere half of 36 per cent = 18 per cent chance of success. It isn't much but there is nothing else to play for.

3. The opening lead is taken with the queen and you set about the hearts by playing the two towards dummy's ... three. If you put up the queen you would have no chance since there is no outside entry to the table. East wins with the nine and returns the six of spades.

You take this with the ace and continue hearts: the eight to West's ten and dummy's queen ... which holds; on the ace both opponents follow, and the rest of the hearts are good.

Bridge is a curious game: in the present example you have to risk not making a heart trick at all (if East has the king), in order to make four.

The Full Deal

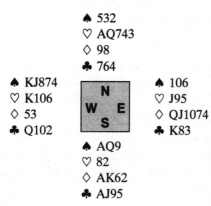

```
                ♠ 532
                ♡ AQ743
                ◊ 98
                ♣ 764
  ♠ KJ874                  ♠ 106
  ♡ K106         N         ♡ J95
  ◊ 53        W     E      ◊ QJ1074
  ♣ Q102         S         ♣ K83
                ♠ AQ9
                ♡ 82
                ◊ AK62
                ♣ AJ95
```

Exercise J

Dealer West. North/South Game.

♠ AK
♡ Q3
◇ A54
♣ AQ10982

♠ 953
♡ K84
◇ Q9873
♣ K7

Lead: ♡J

South	West	North	East
–	1♡	Dble	Pass
1NT	Pass	3NT	All Pass

Preliminary consideration:
Since North/South have 27 points between them, all the outstanding honour cards with the exception perhaps of a knave, must be with the opening bidder.

Questions

1. How many top tricks do you have?

2. How many tricks do you require, and which suit will provide them?

3. What card do you play from dummy on the opening lead?

4. Can you make sure of the contract and if yes, how?

Answers

1. You have 2 in spades, 1 in hearts (after the lead), 1 in diamonds, 3 in clubs = 7 certain tricks.

2. Two extra tricks will suffice and you will look to the club suit for these.

3. West has a heart suit headed by AJ10 and by putting up the queen you will retain a second guard in the suit provided you keep East out of the lead.

4. If the clubs are 3-2 (68 per cent) or the knave of clubs is bare, or West has Jxxx, success is assured, but what will happen if East has Jxxx? You will have to let your right-hand opponent in and his heart return will be fatal.

The solution is simple: after winning the queen of hearts at Trick 1, play the two of clubs of dummy and put in the seven from your hand. If West wins with the knave, the rest of the club suit is established and no return from him can harm you, and if West follows with a small club you will make six club tricks and East will not be able to play a heart through you.

The Full Deal

```
                    ♠ AK
                    ♡ Q3
                    ◇ A54
                    ♣ AQ10982
    ♠ QJ2                           ♠ 108764
    ♡ AJ1092       ┌─────────┐      ♡ 765
    ◇ KJ106        │    N    │      ◇ 2
    ♣ 4            │ W     E │      ♣ J653
                   │    S    │
                   └─────────┘
                    ♠ 953
                    ♡ K84
                    ◇ Q9873
                    ♣ K7
```

Exercise K

Dealer West. East/West Game.

♠ 63
♡ A743
◇ KQJ
♣ AJ108

♠ A109
♡ J105
◇ A1043
♣ 952

Lead: ♠4

South	West	North	East
–	Pass	1♣	Pass
1NT	Pass	2NT	Pass
3NT	All Pass		

Questions

1. How many top tricks?

2. Where will the other tricks come from?

3. Do you duck the opening lead? If yes, how many times? (East will play the knave of spades at Trick 1, and continue with the two.)

4. How will you plan the rest of the play?

Answers

1. 1 in spades, 1 in hearts, 4 in diamonds, 1 in clubs = 7 sure tricks. You require two more.

2. The hearts are not very attractive for a suit such as Axxx opposite J10x will never bring in three tricks. In clubs, on the other hand, you possess all the intermediates down to the eight. The knave and ten accompanying the ace, you will make three tricks 75 per cent of the time.

3. The Rule of 7 would suggest that you should duck twice (7 − 5 = 2) and indeed this would be essential if the spades were breaking 5-3. However, there are further considerations on this deal. In order to take two finesses in the club suit you will need two entries to your hand. If you duck two spades and West switches to a red suit you will be in trouble. East's return of the two of spades suggests that he started with either two or four cards so either way you can afford to play the ace on the second round.

4. How do you handle the club suit? The success of your contract will depend on your answer to this question.

    You may be inclined to begin with the nine from hand but after the first finesse has lost to East you will be obliged to return to hand to take it again. If West began with four clubs to an honour you will be unable to capture it for lack of a further entry to your hand and the clubs will bring you two tricks only.

    The correct way consists in playing the two to dummy's ten on the first round and later the nine to dummy's eight, thereby retaining the lead in your hand for a third finesse towards AJ.

The Full Deal

```
                    ♠ 63
                    ♡ A743
                    ◇ KQJ
                    ♣ AJ108
      ♠ KQ74        ┌─────────┐      ♠ J852
      ♡ KQ9         │    N    │      ♡ 862
      ◇ 52          │ W     E │      ◇ 9876
      ♣ Q763        │    S    │      ♣ K4
                    └─────────┘
                    ♠ A109
                    ♡ J105
                    ◇ A1043
                    ♣ 952
```

Exercise L

Dealer South. Love All.

♠ K4
♡ KQ53
♡ AKJ
♣ QJ73

```
    N
  W   E
    S
```

♠ A93
♡ J102
◇ Q542
♣ 1064

Lead: ♠Q

South	West	North	East
Pass	1♠	Dble	Pass
1NT	Pass	3NT	All Pass

Questions

1. How many top tricks?

2. Which suit will you establish?

3. Do you duck the opening lead? (Perhaps this question is not so simple as it appears if the defence is perfect.)

Answers

1. 2 in spades, 4 in diamonds = 6 tricks.

2. The three extra tricks will come from hearts, you just have to knock out the ace.

3. You hold two spade stoppers and intend to give up the lead only once (with the ace of hearts); the duck is therefore unnecessary, perhaps it is even harmful, since you will only make four diamond tricks by unblocking the AKJ. If the suit is 4-2 (48 per cent) you will not be able to overtake the knave without sacrificing a trick.

See what will happen if you win the first trick with the king of spades as you may well be inclined to do in such a situation: you unblock the diamonds and play a heart to the ten which holds, cash the queen of diamonds and then continue to establish the hearts. West wins the third round of hearts and plays on spades. You will have no entry to the table to cash your thirteenth heart. So this solution is clearly unsatisfactory.

Now consider taking the lead with the ace of spades. You unblock the diamonds and play a heart to your ten. West cannot prevent you from reaching your hand to cash the queen of diamonds, and the king of spades remains on the table as access to the dummy's fourth heart.

NB. If you had ducked the first round of spades, you could have said goodbye to your entry to the good heart.

The Full Deal

```
                ♠ K4
                ♡ KQ53
                ♡ AKJ
                ♣ QJ73
  ♠ QJ1087     ┌─────────┐    ♠ 652
  ♡ A64        │    N    │    ♡ 987
  ◇ 96         │ W     E │    ◇ 10873
  ♣ AK5        │    S    │    ♣ 982
               └─────────┘
                ♠ A93
                ♡ J102
                ◇ Q542
                ♣ 1064
```

As soon as the opening lead has been made you should not fail to take account of any communications problems which might occur.

Exercise M

Dealer East. East/West Game.

```
              ♠ Q42
              ♡ KQ7
              ◊ KQ6
              ♣ A1093
```

```
              ♠ KJ10
              ♡ A98
              ◊ A108
              ♣ KQ65
```

Lead: ♠9

South	West	North	East
–	–	–	Pass
1NT	Pass	4NT	Pass
6NT	All Pass		

East wins the spade lead with the ace and continues with the six.

Questions

1. How many tricks are lacking?

2. What is the only danger?

3. How will you overcome that obstacle?

4. Will your chosen technique be infallible?

Answers

1. You have 2 spades, 3 hearts, 3 diamonds and 3 clubs. That leaves you with one trick to find.

2. You can only establish the twelfth trick in clubs; if the suit breaks 3-2, no problem, but if it is 4-1 (28 per cent) you will have to guess which opponent holds Jxxx.

3. Whenever you are faced with this type of dilemma, there is a
    technique which should occur to you automatically: a count of the
    hand. You cash all your winners in the other three suits, for the
    discards furnished by your opponents (as well as those not played)
    will provide you with the solution.

A third round of spades reveals that West began with five, for East
discards a diamond. Three rounds of hearts follow and again on the
third round East discards a diamond. East's two major-suit doubletons
reveal that West began with ten cards in spades and hearts. He
therefore cannot have more than three cards in the minors. You now
cash your diamond winners to find out the exact distribution. West
follows twice but on the third round he discards the seven of spades.
The composition of both hands in now known. West cannot have more
than one club. Cash the ace in case West's singleton is the knave. No,
he plays the four. Now lead the ten and run it if East fails to cover. The
slam is yours.

The Full Deal

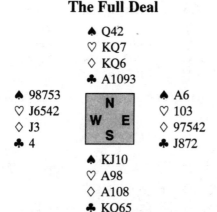

```
                ♠ Q42
                ♡ KQ7
                ◇ KQ6
                ♣ A1093
  ♠ 98753                    ♠ A6
  ♡ J6542        N           ♡ 103
  ◇ J3        W     E        ◇ 97542
  ♣ 4            S           ♣ J872
                ♠ KJ10
                ♡ A98
                ◇ A108
                ♣ KQ65
```

Only one situation would leave you in doubt, and that is when both
opponents followed to three rounds of spades, hearts and diamonds.
Unless you were able to diagnose correctly from the manner in which each
opponent followed suit the number of cards he began with, you would
have no certain way of finding out if either began with four clubs.

Exercise N

Dealer East. Love All.

♠ KJ2
♡ QJ1063
◇ 95
♣ 1072

♠ A95
♡ 92
◇ AK104
♣ AK63

Lead: ♠7

South	West	North	East
–	–	–	Pass
1♣	Pass	1♡	Pass
2NT	Pass	3♣(i)	Pass
3NT	All Pass		

(i)   Looking for three-card heart support

Questions

1. How many top tricks do you have?

2. Which suit will provide the extra tricks?

3. What inference do you draw from the lead? Which card should you play at Trick 1?

Answers

1. 2 in spades, probably 3, 2 in diamonds, 2 in clubs = 6 tricks. Three more are required.

2. You must set up the hearts. However you must realise that your opponents, who are good defenders, will refuse to win the first round. They will be anxious to cut your communications and consequently you

will require two further entries in the North hand: one to knock out the defence's second heart winner and one to reach the established tricks.

3.   West has led the seven of spades (his fourth best); the Rule of 11 provides you with useful information: 11 - 7 = 4. There are four cards higher than the seven in the North, East and South hands. Well, they are all on view and it is easy to conclude that East has no card higher than the seven. Indeed, he plays the six on the opening lead.

Now remember that two entries are indispensable for the heart establishment. You should now know enough to play the correct card from your hand at Trick 1: not the nine of spades, as your instinct for economy tells you to, but the ace. Thus you will be able to reach the table twice, once by finessing the knave and later with the king.

The Full Deal

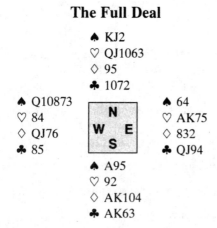

```
              ♠ KJ2
              ♡ QJ1063
              ◇ 95
              ♣ 1072
♠ Q10873      ┌──────┐      ♠ 64
♡ 84          │   N  │      ♡ AK75
◇ QJ76        │ W   E│      ◇ 832
♣ 85          │   S  │      ♣ QJ94
              └──────┘
              ♠ A95
              ♡ 92
              ◇ AK104
              ♣ AK63
```

Exercise 0

Dealer North. Game All.

♠ 763
♡ J105
◇ AQ86
♣ Q42

♠ AK5
♡ K96
◇ K43
♣ A873

Lead: ♠10

South	West	North	East
–	–	Pass	1♠
1NT	Pass	3NT	All Pass

East overtakes the lead of the ten of spades with the knave.

Questions

1. How many tricks do you have initially?

2. What do you know about the position of the missing points?

3. Do you duck the opening lead?

4. How will you play if diamonds turn out to be 4-2?

Answers

1. 2 in spades, 3 in diamonds, 1 in clubs = 6 tricks.

2. Since you have 26 points between your two hands, the king of clubs, ace and queen of hearts and queen and knave of spades are marked with East.

3. The duck, whose main function is to cut communications between defenders, is pointless when all the honour strength lies in the same hand. It can even be fatal, for it can deprive declarer of the opportunity

to put a defender on lead later in the play. Consequently, you win the spade at Trick 1, preserving the five as a potential exit-card.

4. You must set up two heart tricks by finessing for the queen. A 3-3 diamond break will furnish the ninth trick.

At Trick 2 cross to the queen of diamonds and lead the knave of hearts: East goes in with the ace and returns the queen of spades; win with the king (West playing the four), and continue with two further rounds of diamonds. Unfortunately on the ace East discards the five of clubs. On the ten of hearts which follows East plays the queen and on your next heart he discards another club.

You now know the opener's hand: five spades, two hearts, two diamonds and four clubs; put him in with your remaining spade and he will have to yield the ninth trick by leading away from his king of clubs at Trick 12.

The Full Deal

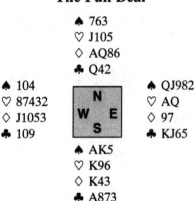

```
                ♠ 763
                ♡ J105
                ◇ AQ86
                ♣ Q42
  ♠ 104                        ♠ QJ982
  ♡ 87432         N            ♡ AQ
  ◇ J1053     W       E        ◇ 97
  ♣ 109           S            ♣ KJ65
                ♠ AK5
                ♡ K96
                ◇ K43
                ♣ A873
```

Exercise P

Dealer South. Love All.

♠ 64
♡ 842
◇ A9852
♣ AKQ

♠ A95
♡ AJ5
◇ QJ103
♣ J103

Lead: ♡K

South	West	North	East
1◇	1V	2♣(i)	Pass
2NT	Pass	3◇(ii)	Pass
3NT	All Pass		

(i)   Too strong for immediate diamond support
(ii) Forcing

Preliminary consideration:

West possesses at least five hearts headed by the king-queen, therefore East has two at most. East is the only defender who can regain the lead (with the king of diamonds).

Questions

1. How many tricks do you have?

2. Which suit will you establish?

3. Do you duck the opening lead? (What is this coup called?)

4. If you decide to duck, is there not the danger of a switch?

5. What solution have you discovered?

6. Will your play succeed against perfect defence?

Answers

1.   1 in spades, 1 in hearts, 1 in diamonds, 3 in clubs = 6 tricks.

2.   Obviously you will go for the diamonds.

3.   If you win the opening lead immediately and the diamond finesse fails, your knave of hearts will be captured by finesse when East returns his partner's suit. You must therefore duck the opening lead. A reminder that this is called the Bath Coup in this situation.

4.   What will happen if you play the five on West's king? He will certainly not continue into your AJ, and he will almost certainly switch to a spade, a suit in which you have only five cards and a single stopper.

5.   You must therefore not only duck the king of hearts, but induce West to continue with the suit. Have you found it? Just contribute your knave without hesitation. In this way you will mask the five of hearts and West will think that his partner has it. He will triumphantly set up his suit by playing another round and you will take your ace and run the queen of diamonds in peace. If East can win this trick you can sit back and enjoy West's discomfort as he waits in vain for the heart return.

6.   The answer to this question is no, for really good defenders note the cards contributed by their partners with the greatest care. If East/West are playing distributional signals throughout East's seven of hearts will be a clear indication to West that your heart holding is AJx and he will certainly find the deadly switch.

The Full Deal

```
                  ♠ 64
                  ♡ 842
                  ◇ A9852
                  ♣ AKQ
   ♠ KQ7          ┌───────┐       ♠ J10832
   ♡ KQ1093       │   N   │       ♡ 76
   ◇ 76           │ W   E │       ◇ K4
   ♣ 842          │   S   │       ♣ 9765
                  └───────┘
                  ♠ A95
                  ♡ AJ5
                  ◇ QJ103
                  ♣ J103
```

Exercise Q

Dealer West. East/West Game.

♠ A102
♡ AK
♢ AQJ64
♣ J95

```
      N
  W       E
      S
```

♠ J84
♡ J75
♢ 32
♣ KQ1086

Lead: ♡4

South	West	North	East
–	Pass	1◊	Pass
1NT	Pass	3NT	All Pass

East plays the two of hearts at Trick 1, playing distributional signals.

Questions

1. How many top tricks?

2. Which suits will provide the extra tricks?

3. In which order will you play them?

Answers

1. 1 in spades, 2 in hearts, 1 in diamonds = 4 tricks. Five more are required.

2. The clubs will furnish four tricks, but as you do not possess any entry to your hand, the defence will hold up twice and kill the suit. The diamonds are a possibility. If West has the doubleton king or even Kxxx you will establish three tricks. If he has Kxx you will make all five diamonds. You will obviously play twice from your hand towards AQJ.

The chance of making an extra trick from the spade suit is so thin that it is not worth considering.

3. After these preliminary analyses you play a club to your hand at Trick 2 and as foreseen nobody wants to take the ace. You now play a diamond to the knave which holds.

Return to hand with the king of clubs (East still cannot go in with the ace without setting up the rest of your clubs) and repeat the diamond finesse; now cash the ace of diamonds (East discards) and play a further round to West. Your fifth diamond is now established as the ninth trick: one spade, two hearts, four diamonds and two clubs.

You will not have failed to notice that it would have been absurd to play a further round of clubs, since your hand was entryless.

The Full Deal

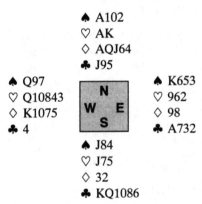

```
              ♠ A102
              ♡ AK
              ◇ AQJ64
              ♣ J95
♠ Q97                        ♠ K653
♡ Q10843         N           ♡ 962
◇ K1075        W   E         ◇ 98
♣ 4              S           ♣ A732
              ♠ J84
              ♡ J75
              ◇ 32
              ♣ KQ1086
```

Exercise R

Dealer West. Love All.

♠ 93
♡ AK64
◇ 953
♣ KQJ2

```
    N
W       E
    S
```

♠ KJ5
♡ 532
◇ AJ4
♣ A763

Lead: ♠7. East plays the queen

South	West	North	East
–	Pass	1♣	Pass
1◇	1♠	Pass	Pass
3NT	All Pass		

Questions

1. How many top tricks?

2. Do you duck East's queen of spades?

3. Which defender must you keep off lead?

4. Which suit will you set up?

5. What technique will you employ?

Answers

1. 1 in spades (after the lead), 2 in hearts, 1 in diamonds, 4 in clubs = 8 tricks. You require only one more.

2. You might think about ducking the queen of spades but this would only be effective if (a) the spades were 6-2; (b) you were certain that only East could regain the lead. The 5-3 break is three times more likely (47 per cent), and West, who clearly holds the ace of spades,

only needs to duck once in order to maintain communication with his partner; if East gains the lead your position will be hopeless.

Consequently, you must win with the king of spades at Trick 1; you still retain a guard with your J5.

3. East is the dangerous opponent since if he regains the lead your ♠Jx will be captured by finesse.

4. The diamond suit is totally unattractive and your only hope of nine tricks lies in a 3-3 heart break. You must set up the six of hearts.

5. However, as it is essential that East does not regain the lead, you must hope that West has ♡Qxx.

In order to make sure that he does not unblock that honour you must play twice towards the ace and king. If West plays the queen on either of your small heart leads, leave him in possession of the trick.

The Full Deal

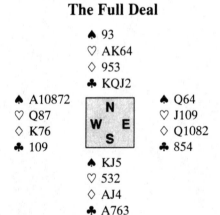

```
              ♠ 93
              ♡ AK64
              ◇ 953
              ♣ KQJ2
  ♠ A10872        N        ♠ Q64
  ♡ Q87                    ♡ J109
  ◇ K76      W       E     ◇ Q1082
  ♣ 109            S       ♣ 854
              ♠ KJ5
              ♡ 532
              ◇ AJ4
              ♣ A763
```

One final word ....

Throughout this book it has been suggested that the defenders are leading 4th best. Here are one or two comments concerning the growing popularity of distributional leads (3rd and 5th).

(a)   With five cards or three the lowest card is led: K7653
(b)   With four cards the third highest is led: K862

Instead of applying the Rule of 11 you apply:

(a)   The Rule of 10 in the case of 5th highest;
(b)   The Rule of 12 in the case of 3rd highest.

Naturally the inferences are clear: the lead of a small card will be more frequently from a five-card suit, and a middle card will more probably be from four cards.